In the Spirit

OTHER WORKS
BY

Wendy Weir

. . .

PANTHER DREAM:
A Story of the African Rainforest

BARU BAY: AUSTRALIA

In the Spirit

CONVERSATIONS WITH

THE SPIRIT OF

JeRRy GaRcia

Wendy Weir

HARMONY BOOKS
NEW YORK

Published by Harmony Books,
201 East 50th Street, New York, New York 10022.
Member of the Crown Publishing Group.

Random House, Inc. New York, Toronto, London, Sydney, Auckland
www.randomhouse.com

Harmony Books is a registered trademark and Harmony Books
colophon is a trademark of Random House, Inc.

Printed in the United States of America

Design by LYNNE AMFT

Library of Congress Cataloging-in-Publication Data
Weir, Wendy, 1949–
In the spirit : conversations with the spirit of Jerry Garcia /
by Wendy Weir.
1. Garcia, Jerry, 1942– (Spirit) 2. Spirit writings.
I. Garcia, Jerry, 1942– (Spirit) II. Title.
BF1311.G35W45 1999
133.9'3—dc21   99-11236
                                                CIP

ISBN 0-609-60461-9

10 9 8 7 6 5 4 3 2 1

First Edition

To all who love Jerry.
To all Jerry loves.

To Dan Laing,
whose spirit in life
shines through his death
and lights our hearts.

Seek the dying star.
Speak out loud
the prayers held deeply in your heart.
They shall be answered.

acknowledgments

Many people have helped me in the creation of this book, and so have many spirits. It does not matter whether their assistance is visible or not; what matters is the thought, the love, and the support that I have received and for which I am deeply grateful.

First of all, I would like to thank my brothers, Bob and John. Words cannot describe the depth of our love, expressed or not, and the knowledge that no matter what happens in life, we are there for each other. My brother Bob has given me many wonderful opportunities to participate in his adventures, and in return, he has shared in mine. This book is one of them. My brother John has often soothed my soul with his quiet, gentle ways and open heart.

In addition, I would like to acknowledge the unconditional support of my close friends and loved ones, some of whom also assisted with this book. They listened to my fears, offered me wise counsel and an occasional escape, and let me do what I needed to do with kind understanding. They are: Liz and Jim Smith, Ellen and Gerry Harden, Milena and Jack Parber, Natascha Muenter, Linda Jay Brandt, Andrew Wernick, David Tarai Roland, and Yemeh. I would also like to thank Tiff Garcia, Jerry's brother, who, with his heartfelt encouragement and enthusiasm for the project, removed any concerns I had about publishing this material.

I am greatly appreciative to those friends who contributed

directly to this book. Robert Hunter generously gave me permission to use his lyrics, and Alan Trist from Ice Nine Publishing read each song to make sure that it was rendered correctly. Frances Shurtliff reviewed the book for content and accuracy, offering me her warm support and valuable advice. Stacy Kreutzmann Quinn, Bruce Scotton, Debbi Lerman, Toby McLeod, Jessica Abbe, and Milena Parber offered constructive editorial advice on the early drafts. Tom Stack reviewed the illustrations for accuracy, and Linda Jay Brandt did an excellent job proofing the final copy. Dennis McNally, the Grateful Dead publicist, patiently and thoroughly answered all of my Dead-related questions. Aboriginal artist Terry Yumbulul created the prototype for my illustration of Baru, the Crocodile, accompanying Chapter 17. Jaichima and Vicente gave me permission to publish what I wrote about them. This is the first time that such permission has been granted, and I am deeply honored by their trust and confidence.

My thanks to Natascha Muenter, who collaborated with me on the Message from the Dying Star. I had a vision of this image as a symbol for the book when I first started writing but I didn't know what it meant. A year and a half later, Natascha heard the message in a dream and, unbeknownst to her, the symbol for the Dying Star was the same as my illustration. Together, my image and her dream complete the Message.

I would like to thank my literary agent, Sarah Lazin. Her friendship of ten years, her in-depth knowledge of the rock and roll scene, and her professional publishing expertise were invaluable in the formation, writing, and rewriting of this manuscript. I am also grateful to my editor, Shaye Areheart, and to the staff at Harmony Books for sharing in my vision with their editorial comments, the dynamic cover design, and the teamwork needed to produce and promote this work.

Most of all, I wish to acknowledge all of you who read this book. The connection goes both ways: as I enrich your life, so you enrich mine. May your journey be filled with joy and love, humor and wisdom, and may you sing your own song for all of us to hear.

contents

contents

book two 1996
july 10—august 11

List of Lyrics

List of iLLustrations

Lady with a Fan

Excerpt from lyrics by Robert Hunter

Let my inspiration flow
in token lines suggesting rhythm
that will not forsake me
till my tale is told and done

while the firelight's aglow
strange shadows in the flames will grow
till things we've never seen
will seem familiar

the storyteller makes no choice
soon you will not hear his voice
his job is to shed light
and not to master

In the Spirit

JERRY AND ME

preface

THIS IS NOT A BOOK ABOUT THE MAN JERRY GARCIA—
lead guitarist for the legendary rock and roll band the Grateful
Dead—who died on August 9, 1995, at the age of fifty-three. This is
a book about his spirit. This is also a book about me, Wendy Weir,
sister of Bob Weir, rhythm guitarist for the Grateful Dead.

You might think that growing up with a brother in the Grateful
Dead would mean that I was a hippie in the Sixties and followed the
band around the country like many of its followers, known as
Deadheads. Actually, the exact opposite is true. As children, Bob was
the "rebel." I was the "perfect child." He spoke out. I was quiet and
agreeable. We both had the same upbringing, but we strove for love
and attention in diametrically opposed ways.

When Bob started playing with Jerry and the other members of
the band in 1965, I was in a private girls' school. I graduated in 1966
and went to college at the University of California, Berkeley. I loved
learning and studied hard, graduating with a history major when I
was twenty. The closest I got to the Vietnam protests was walking
through clouds of tear gas on my way to class. I was a pacifist.

After graduation, I entered the world of financial marketing.
Over the past twenty-five years, I have been a bank vice president,
administrator of a bank insurance nonprofit organization, and a

financial marketing consultant. I still work on a consulting basis in the area of export trade finance.

But the world of finance is only a part of my interests. I have also studied spirituality and energetic healing and explored my own psychic abilities, which I first became aware of when I was twenty-one. I have expressed my artistic and literary talents in partnership with Bob through the creation of our environmental children's books with narration and music, *Panther Dream: A Story of the African Rainforest* and *Baru Bay: Australia.* And I am an environmental educator, a cofounder and former executive director of Coral Forest (a nonprofit organization dedicated to the preservation of coral reefs around the world through education and grassroots action), and, along with Bob, a director of Reef Relief in Key West, Florida, where we are expanding our coral reef and rainforest education efforts and activities.

The Grateful Dead is also a part of me. For thirty years, they have been my family, a warm, loving extension of my sibling relationship with Bob. I must confess, I would never have gone to a Grateful Dead show if I hadn't been related to Bob. I have grown to love the music, but I really went to the shows for the people, to be with my family and friends, to share in the excitement of the crowd, to wander through the aisles and see people who are truly happy, if only for a few hours.

Last and probably most important of all, I love life and nature: riding my horse, walking through the redwood forest or along a beach with my loved one, sitting peacefully under the night sky looking up at the vast array of stars. Here I am one with my surroundings, a part of the rhythm of the Universe. My outer world blends with my inner one and I feel complete.

This book started unexpectedly with a simple phone call from Bob on the morning of Jerry's death. He asked me to check in telepathically with Jerry's spirit to find out why he had passed on and how he was doing. Bob and I had done this several times before with the passing of dear friends, so I did not think of it as anything special, let alone the harbinger of personal change, yet harbinger it was.

Change is never easy, and this has certainly been true of the changes that I went through during my communications with Jerry's spirit and in the writing of this book. Oh, the channeling part was easy because all I had to do was get ready and take dictation, but the personal part was far more challenging, because in order to understand and write about it, I had to confront some of my own fears. I had not expected this, but there they were, staring me in the face, demanding my attention. At first I hoped that these fears would disappear, or at least fade away, so I wouldn't have to look at them, but that didn't happen. Then I tried to avoid them by creating excuses: I wouldn't release this information until I was ready, the time was right, I had more time to work on it, and so on. All of this was valid, but eventually I had to stop and look. And look again. My fears had come out of hiding and stood squarely on the path in front of me. I had run out of detours. There was no other way but to walk forward and greet them as best I could.

The first fear was that people would think I was crazy. As I approached it, I could hear the voices of faceless people talking in my head, saying, "This is ridiculous! How can she communicate with Jerry Garcia? He's dead. Anyway, what does he know? He was on drugs a lot. She's just doing it for the publicity." And then other voices would join in, saying, "I always thought Wendy was so nice and reasonable. How do we know she's really talking with his spirit?"

You see, throughout my life, from childhood until recently, I have sought people's love by being the "good little girl," by doing what was expected of me, pleasing them in order to feel pleased with myself. This worked very effectively until a few weeks after the end of the channeling sessions, when I came to the subtle yet life-altering realization that it was time to go deep, very deep, within to remember who I truly am, not who I thought I should be. It has been an intense two-year journey, filled with the pain of breaking down and releasing old belief systems and structures that no longer work, and the joy of creating a new life within myself where I am free and whole.

By publishing this information, I know that I am no longer going to be perceived as the "good little girl," and I now accept the fact that it is okay to be loved for myself. What helped me a lot throughout this transition was the love and support of my brother Bob, my family, and my close friends. They would be there, saying, "Go for it! We are glad someone is finally talking about the spiritual side, the positive side, of Jerry and the band."

Standing next to this fear was a second one: Would people think that I was capitalizing on Jerry's death? This is a very sensitive subject with Bob, me, and many of the immediate Grateful Dead family. We feel very strongly that it would lessen our integrity, demean our individual selves, if we were to do something so base as to benefit from a dear friend's death. That is not what family is about. That is not what friendship is about.

Bob and I talked about this issue for a long time. He was clear that he would not actively participate in writing the book because he did not want to profit in any way from Jerry's death. I understood and agreed with him, but for me it was different. This was my experience. This was my truth. And whenever my fears started to cloud the picture, Jerry's spirit would appear, pushing and prodding me to publish this information so that it could reach as many people as possible. The motive, he reminded me, was not to profit. It was to help.

It took a lot of soul-diving, but at last I am clear: It is not what other people think of me, it is what I think of myself. One of my passions and gifts is to help others heal, which also helps to heal me. That's a part of who I am, a healer. I am also a published author and illustrator. I get paid for my work. This is an important concept to accept, because if I don't get paid for my time and talent, then I can't pay my bills and support myself. And if I can't help myself, then I can't help others.

Close behind the first two fears stood a third one: that people were going to go around saying they channel Jerry Garcia like some people channel Merlin, the Sorcerer. I could just see a listing in *Common Ground,* our local New Age magazine:

> I channel Jerry Garcia. Learn his wisdom for the evolution and unfolding of your own spiritual path. Private sessions held in tie-dyed office with music by the Grateful Dead playing softly in the background. To understand what a long, strange trip this has been, contact Sunshine Daydream.

Actually, I didn't have a problem with the above statement. Except for the tie-dyed office, softly playing Grateful Dead music, and Sunshine Daydream, these words pretty much apply to this book. What I did have a problem with was the thought that I might be creating a situation that some people can take advantage of, misuse, or misrepresent—for profit or not. I have always been extremely responsible, and the thought of someone using this information irresponsibly bothered me a great deal. Also, I didn't like losing control of myself or a situation, and to move forward with this meant I would have to let go. Now, after two years, I have arrived at the point where I am not only able to let go, I am able to laugh when I think of all the possible scenarios this information might create.

The last fear on my path did not stand in front of me but danced all around. The white brittle bones of its skeleton would creak and clack, distracting my attention. One moment I would see it and think I understood, and the next moment it would dissolve and reappear in a place I was not looking. Initially I recognized the skeleton as my fear of death, which surprised me. Having experienced the deaths of my parents and other loved ones, and because of my involvement in the process of death and dying from a healing perspective, I thought that I was comfortable with the idea of my own death. But in the channeled communications of August 28, 1995, I learned that this comfort was on an intellectual and spiritual level, not a physical and emotional one. Somewhere deep inside all of us is the primal instinct and desire to survive, and walking hand in hand with this is the fear—and knowledge—that we won't.

Once I came to this realization, the skeleton stopped moving and I could gaze clearly into the dark, spacious cavities of its eyes. I saw and felt a vast, empty void beckoning me to pass through these vacant sockets, and from the depth of my being rose the greatest fear of all: dissolving into nothingness, death of the self. My ego cried out to me, trying to stop me from entering, but I would not turn aside. I moved through the portals of the skull and in the darkness I found life.

Even after befriending these fears, though, I was still indecisive about publishing this material. What finally convinced me to move forward was not that this channeled information had to be released because it was new or unique. It is actually similar to the teachings of Christ, Buddha, and other enlightened Masters. It was the constant pressure, on a spirit level, that the time is now. Not now as in today (this is our understanding of time), but NOW as seen from a cosmic perspective.

Our Earth is changing, life is moving faster, time is shifting. There are crises in the economic, social, political, and religious structures around the world. Our environment is being destroyed at a rate that could threaten the existence of the human race in the next fifty years. Yet there is also a shift in energy. People are becoming more aware that they must first heal themselves before they can heal others. It is for this purpose, to help people heal themselves, that the book is being published NOW. These teachings have been spoken before and they will be spoken again and again and again, in as many different ways and from as many different sources as it takes for us to wake up and live these teachings each and every day of our lives.

The journey is an inner one, where we move through our own heart and into the solar plexus area of our own body. This is the core where our spirit lives. This is our place of true knowing. Our mind might confuse us, our heart overwhelm us, but our core, our gut feelings, will always present us with the TRUTH if only we remember to ask the questions and trust in the answers.

In addition to being the lead guitarist for the Grateful Dead for more than thirty years, Jerry Garcia was well known and well loved as an accomplished musician of other instruments, an amazing artist, and a warm humanitarian. Many of the band's million-plus followers around the world looked at him, if not as the leader of the band, then as the "papa bear." In reality, Jerry was not and never wished to be the leader. All of the original band members were equals. All were leaders. It started that way in 1965 and it remains that way today.

Through his music, his art, his words, and his actions, Jerry was able to communicate with a lot of people in a lot of different ways. He touched them with the reality of his life, its joys and sorrows, triumphs and hardships. He appeared in their dreams and moved in and out of their consciousness. He did this when he was physically alive, and he continues to do this in the spirit. He might even communicate with others in the way that he communicates with me. Jerry was and is a very talented being.

I have divided *In the Spirit* into two parts: Book One and Book Two. Each part can stand alone, yet each is an integral part of the whole and therefore both have been presented together.

Book One consists of my communications with Jerry's spirit in August and September 1995, starting on the day of his death. These conversations have been edited only where it is necessary to protect confidential information or to clarify a point. In this book, I have included pictures, illustrations, and song lyrics to create a "feeling" for each chapter. The lyrics are by Robert Hunter, and most of the music for them was composed by Jerry Garcia, with whom Hunter had a very close creative partnership and friendship. All of these lyrics have been performed by the Grateful Dead in concert.

The word *God* is used throughout this book for the sake of convenience and familiarity. It represents the God/Goddess Force, the Prime Creator, All That Is. It does not represent a God that is male and restricted to certain religions. Likewise, the words *Jerry, he,* and *his* are used throughout this book in reference to Jerry's spirit, even though the spirit is androgynous, being neither male nor female but a blended balance of the two.

Book Two consists of the communications that I had with Jerry's spirit in July and August 1996, surrounding the first anniversary of his death. All was not well on the astral plane and he needed help. At the end of the book he surprises me with a gift. It is a folk tale about the Grateful Dead, but unlike the old folk tales from which the name Grateful Dead was derived, this is a modern tale about the band. I feel that it is important in this day and age that we have our own myths and tales to teach, entertain, and guide us. As the band and its music weaves in and out of our lives, myths weave in and out of time. For each age, they hold a deep and powerful meaning, and just when we think they may no longer apply, we discover a new meaning in their words and a new beginning.

As with a Grateful Dead concert, you may relate to this material immediately, or not at all, or you might need to read it a few times before you understand what it's all about, or you might want to put the book down and come back to it later. Whatever the circumstances, know that within the folds of this book, between the words, the lines, and the spaces, there is a special message for each of you who has the courage to hear it, and *know* that when you are ready, this message will strike truth on the deepest level of your being.

In the spirit,

Wendy Weir
San Rafael, California
May 1998

In the Spirit

IN THE SPIRIT
I WILL WANDER
THROUGH FIELDS OF GOLDEN LIGHT
CLOTHED IN COLORS OF THE UNIVERSE
AND RHYTHMS OF THE NIGHT.

IN THE SPIRIT
I WILL HOLD YOU
AND WHISPER WORDS SO DEAR
TO HELP YOU LOOK WITHIN YOUR HEART AND
LET GO OF ALL YOUR FEAR.

IN THE SPIRIT
WE'LL REMEMBER
OUR TRUE IDENTITY
FOR WE HAVE ALWAYS BEEN ONE IN SPIRIT
THROUGHOUT ETERNITY.

WENDY WEIR

book one

1995

august 9–september 15

i'm quite sure if we start
kicking things around,
if we listen in our hearts and
inside somewhere,
that we'll hear that thread that
we've always heard.
and i'm sure he's still singing.

BOB WEIR
on Jerry Garcia's death
AUGUST 1995

He's Gone

Excerpt from lyrics by Robert Hunter

RAT IN A DRAIN DITCH
CAUGHT ON A LIMB
YOU KNOW BETTER BUT
I KNOW HIM
LIKE I TOLD YOU
WHAT I SAID
STEAL YOUR FACE
RIGHT OFF YOUR HEAD

NOW HE'S GONE
LORD, HE'S GONE
LIKE A STEAM LOCOMOTIVE
ROLLING DOWN THE TRACK
HE'S GONE
HE'S GONE
AND NOTHING'S GONNA BRING HIM BACK
HE'S GONE

The Grateful Dead performed this song in concert to honor the passing of a close friend.

DYING STAR

Death

WEDNESDAY, AUGUST 9, 1995

THE PHONE RINGS. I'M IN THE MIDDLE OF A PLEASANT dream and find it hard to wake up. I force my eyes open and notice that the rays of the rising sun are starting to stream through my window, filling the room with soft, pale light. Rolling over in bed, I pick up the receiver and say hello in a somewhat distant voice.

"Is it true?" It takes a moment before I realize that it's my literary agent, Sarah Lazin, calling from New York.

"Is what true?" I reply groggily, wondering why she is calling me this early in the morning.

"Jerry Garcia is dead," she says softly, with a sense of deep concern and urgency.

"What?" As I start to retrieve my senses, the first thought that comes to me is, No, this is just another rumor. He has been cleaning up, getting off drugs, never looking better. No, this is just another of those silly things that people are saying about the band.

Sarah continues, "I heard it on the news. Is it true?"

"I don't know. Let me call the Dead office and find out. I'll call you back as soon as I can." My voice has regained its clarity although my mind is lagging somewhere behind.

Thoughts run scattered through my head as I dial the Dead office. Rumors, I always seem to be checking out rumors. Oh well, one more time. The line is busy. That's strange, it's never busy. A feeling of concern starts to rise in my body. I try again and can't get through. Something is wrong. Now what? I call Grateful Dead Merchandising because I know they always answer their phone. In response to a strained voice on the other end of the line, I say, "This is Wendy Weir. Can I speak to Patricia?"

Silence, transfer click, silence, then the line picks up. The voice is beyond pain. Before I say, "Hi, Patricia. Is it true?" I know that it is. At the age of fifty-three, Jerry Garcia is dead.

My first response is one of being responsible and organized. Okay, let me think clearly. First I need to call Sarah back and let her know it is true. So I call her and tell her what I heard from Patricia. Then I put down the phone and sit to gather my feelings and thoughts.

My mind races, not wanting to deal with the feeling part deep inside me. Next, I think, I need to call Bob. Then I realize that I can't because he's back East on tour with his band Ratdog, and I don't know if he's on the bus or in a hotel. I'll just have to wait for him to call me. I wonder if he has heard yet.

An hour later, the phone rings. It's Bob. We talk briefly and I ask how he is doing. It's that sisterly concern coming out. Of course, I know he is okay. We have dealt with death before and we know, for ourselves, that death is a transition from the physical to the spiritual. Although the body may come and go, the spirit lives forever. And, as he has done before with the death of a dear friend or loved one, he asks, "Can you check in on Jerry for me and see what's happening?"

"Sure," I reply. "Let me see what I can do."

"I'm flying out after the show tonight and will call you when I get home," he says matter-of-factly. The rest of our exchange is brief and to the point. We have never needed lots of words to communicate. A sense of shock underlies our voices, but now is not the time to talk about it. That will have to wait for when each of us, in our own way, can find the space to deal with what has just happened.

After a few parting words, we hang up, Bob returning to a constant, unrelenting stream of phone calls; I turning off my phone and going into the living room to sit in one of my mother's straight-backed, thinly cushioned Oriental chairs to meditate before contacting Jerry.

Placing my feet flat on the ground, I straighten my back to allow the energies to flow easily up and down my spine, hold my head erect with eyes closed, and rest my hands peacefully on my thighs. I start to inhale slowly through my nose, breathing deeply into my lungs, holding my breath for a few seconds, then exhaling through my mouth. I repeat this several times until my body and mind are fully relaxed. Then I gently shift my focus to the inner space behind my sixth chakra (the energy center located on the forehead just above and between the eyes), clear my head of all thoughts, and raise the frequency of my energy. Entering into a meditative state, I silently call Jerry's name.

Almost instantly, I see Jerry's spirit. It looks like a brilliant, white-gold beam radiating out from a center of pure light. Free at last from the weight and pain of his physical body, he is in a powerful state of ecstasy. It reminds me of an excited young boy who has just run home from his last day of school and is free for summer vacation.

I have reached him on the astral level, which is the plane above the Earth's atmosphere where most spirits from here go after death, either to rest and eventually reincarnate on Earth, or to move on to other dimensions.

The spirit vibrates at its own unique energy level, which serves to identify it. Like fingerprints, no two vibrations are the same. In order to reach an individual spirit, I raise my own vibration and think of the individual I wish to contact, often saying his or her Earth name to set my "channel." Then I transmit my thought waves. The projection of my thoughts establishes the energetic or telepathic link that I need for communication. If the spirit wishes to respond, it sends its thoughts back to me and they enter my brain, where they are translated into words, often taking on a masculine or feminine feeling reflective of the spirit's life on Earth. Since all communication with the spirit world is influenced by the state of the person receiving it, it is important for me to be as clear and precise as possible, and to attain and maintain a very high frequency. Meditation enables me to do this.

Jerry, can you talk with me? I ask. There is no answer, only radiant energy.

Jerry, can you talk with me? I repeat.

From a great distance, I feel him making a tremendous effort to communicate. Instead of a clear response, I hear a soft rumbling, gargled tone and can barely make out his words. I listen more intently. Very, very slowly he mumbles: *I...can't...talk...to...you.*

Why? I hurriedly ask, hoping not to lose the connection. But the voice is gone, only his vision remains. I feel that something is wrong, very wrong.

I hold on to Jerry's vision so that I can understand what is happening. Probing with my thoughts, I feel the awful memory of Earthly pain and an intense desire to escape emanating from his spirit. Now finally free, he doesn't want to return for any reason. But I also sense that if his spirit leaves now before fulfilling its life's mission, this would not serve Jerry's higher purpose.

I try again to communicate with him. He hears me but doesn't want to talk. He just wants to be left alone. How am I going to get through to him? For a moment I hesitate, then I know what to do. I send my thoughts to Bob, asking for his help. His loving bond with

Jerry is unbreakable. If anyone can make a difference, he can. Bob telepathically hears my call and instantly joins his energy with mine. Now we are both fighting, on a higher dimension, to reach Jerry and remind him that he has a commitment to fulfill. He can't just leave.

Time doesn't exist. All that exists is the struggle. Jerry is angry and won't let us near. He doesn't want anything to do with the Earth. All he remembers at this moment is the pain and all he wants to do is escape from it. Like sitting with a loved one who has been badly hurt, we feel his anguish and offer him our support, yet we stay firm in the truth that it is important for him to fulfill his Earthly mission.

Again and again, Bob and I project our thoughts straight to Jerry, but they have no effect, silently disappearing into the cottonlike clouds surrounding the walls of his energy field. As we look at each other, we suddenly realize that the path to Jerry is not a direct one. We must go above his barriers and contact his spirit on a higher plane of consciousness, where it is no longer clogged with fear and pain. Moving upward with our vibration, we sense the walls becoming thinner and thinner. Finally we are able to push through into his awareness, holding the image of our loving, safe embrace in our thoughts.

Slowly, very slowly, his defenses begin to relax and we feel his growing awareness of a deeper truth within. Slowly, very slowly, he begins to remember his purpose on Earth and the importance of completing it before moving on. A sense of resigned humor gradually replaces his anger and frustration as he turns his attention to us. A slight mischievous smile radiates outward as if to say, "Oh well, I almost made it!"

Jerry's spirit softly embraces Bob's and mine as a way of thanking us for staying with him through the struggle. We are all psychically exhausted, yet happy. The bonds of love have remained unbroken. Jerry is still with us and ready to communicate, this time in the spirit.

I gradually come out of my meditative state. I am too tired to try talking with Jerry again, so I decide to wait until early tomorrow morning when I am rested and clear.

Now, you may be wondering: How can I talk with spirits? The answer is simple: We all can. The explanation, however, is much more complicated, because in order to understand what is about to happen, you must first understand who I am and what I believe.

Playing in the Band

Excerpt from lyrics by Robert Hunter

some folks trust to reason
others trust to might
i don't trust to nothing
but i know it come out right

say it once again now
oh, i hope you understand
when it's done and over
lord, a man is just a man

playing
playing in the band
daybreak
daybreak on the land

some folks look for answers
others look for fights
some folks up in treetops
just look to see the sights

i can tell your future
look what's in your hand
but i can't stop for nothing
i'm just playing in the band

OUR NEW HOME

CHAPTER 2

Growing Up

ALL OF US, AS HUMAN BEINGS, HAVE SPECIAL INTU-
itive and creative abilities, although some of us may not be consciously aware of them. I, for one, was not aware of mine when I was
growing up.

By all accounts, I had a very good childhood, what I thought of
as normal. I was born in October 1949 into a family that already had
two brothers. The older one was John, born in April 1945, and the
younger one was Bob, born in October 1947. When I was nine
months old, our parents, Eleanor and Fred, moved us from San
Francisco to a new home in Atherton, about thirty miles south. There
we grew up in a peaceful, beautiful environment, surrounded by lawn
and trees, and joined by our family dog.

All three of us children went to Selby Lane, the local elementary
school. Our young lives consisted primarily of school; playing with our
friends and dogs; horseback riding for me; and teasing one another.

Sometimes Bob and John would build a cardboard house and
convince me to go inside, only to crash it down upon me once I was
in there. I was never hurt, only scared, and for some inexplicable
reason I kept trusting my brothers and going back for more. To this

day, I still trust both of them very deeply, but at the same time, I *have* learned how to defend myself!

When I was nine years old, I got my first horse, Mister Bay, and if I wasn't doing my homework from school, I was riding or drawing pictures of horses. I always thought of artists as being driven to draw, yet I was never passionate about it. I just did it for fun. Over the years, I often asked myself: "Why were you born with this natural talent? What are you going to do with it?" And my response was always: "I don't know."

When I was eleven, a friend of our parents' spent the weekend and brought his guitar. Bob played it for the first time and never put it down. He was hooked. I also started seventh grade that year at a private girls' school, Crystal Springs. I had had enough of boys.

When I was thirteen, John graduated from high school and joined the army. Bob, who finished his sophomore year at Fountain Valley School in Colorado (where he became best friends with his future songwriter, John Barlow) and was asked not to return because he was slightly nonconformist, started his junior year at our local public high school, where he was accompanied daily by his guitar. Both of our parents had their own businesses and, looking back, I wonder when our mother ever had any time for herself. If she wasn't at her office in San Francisco, she was driving me to the stables or Bob to Dana Morgan's music store in Palo Alto, where he played with the store's guitar teacher, Jerry Garcia.

When I was fourteen, life changed. It was the summer of 1964. One bright, warm Sunday morning our mother returned from church and with our father asked Bob and me to join them outside for a talk (John was still in the army, stationed in Germany). This seemed strange because we were not a family that "talked" together. It was then that we learned that our mother, at the age of forty-five, had breast cancer. Although she was very positive about healing, she knew that she would be fighting for her life and she wanted us to understand. In those days if you had cancer, it was tantamount to a death sentence, and so for the first time, the insecurity of the unknown and the presence of death became a part of our daily lives. The safe, stable childhood that I had known came to an end. I felt that I was now an adult dealing with adult issues.

Around this time, the presence of death came into our lives in another way as well. Bob had been playing with Jerry Garcia in a jug band, Mother McCree's Uptown Jug Champions. Bob played the gut bucket (he referred to it as washtub bass), the jug, and the washboard, all of which held prominent places in his bedroom between gigs. Jerry played the banjo. They were doing well, but when the Beatles hit the scene big-time, the jug band decided to go electric. In 1965 they formed a rock and roll band with Pigpen called the Warlocks. Soon Bill Kreutzmann and Phil Lesh joined them. Occasionally the five band members—Jerry on lead guitar, Bob on rhythm guitar, Phil on bass, Pigpen on keyboard, and Billy on drums—would practice at our house. If I was home, I would stop and listen. Being both older and boys, they often liked to tease me and called me "Bob's little sister" or "little sis." My name, Wendy, did not exist in their vocabulary.

Then one evening at dinner, which was really Bob's breakfast, since he was out all night playing music and home all day sleeping, he announced that they had heard there was another band back East called the Warlocks. Since they were planning to go national, they had to change their name. They were now going to call themselves the Grateful Dead. For a brief moment there was silence, then Mom, Dad, and I said all at once, "Yuk, what an awful name! Why do you want to call yourselves that? It's too weird and morbid. You can't be serious!"

But Bob was serious. Realizing that we weren't going to change his mind, our mother looked at the large antique painting of five Tibetan deities that hung on the dining room wall behind us and said, "These are the Grateful Dead." I have often wondered if her words were merely poetic.

A Touch of Grey

Excerpt from lyrics by Robert Hunter

DAWN IS BREAKING EVERYWHERE
LIGHT A CANDLE, CURSE THE GLARE
DRAW THE CURTAINS
I DON'T CARE 'CAUSE
IT'S ALL RIGHT

I WILL GET BY
I WILL GET BY
I WILL GET BY
I WILL SURVIVE

SORRY THAT YOU FEEL THAT WAY
THE ONLY THING THERE IS TO SAY
EVERY SILVER LINING'S GOT A
TOUCH OF GREY

I WILL GET BY
I WILL GET BY
I WILL GET BY
I WILL SURVIVE

CONTACT

C H A P T E R   3

Reality Shifts

WHAT HAPPENS IN PEOPLE'S LIVES TO ALTER THEIR view of reality? Usually it is a traumatic experience, such as the death of a loved one, a divorce, the loss of a job, or a move. Occasionally it is an ecstatic experience, such as the birth of one's child or the feeling of love. Sometimes, it is a combination of the two.

Looking back, I realize there have been many incredible experiences, both painful and joyous, that have influenced who I am today. However, three stand out as heralding major turning points in my life: the death of my parents, my divorce, and Otis.

It is early March 1971. I am twenty-one years old. My mother has just died from cancer and I have finished making arrangements for her cremation. I am at home with my father, who is in the final stages of his cancer. He decided a few months ago that he did not want to live without my mother and so he contracted this disease. Bob and John have been helping out as much as possible, but today I am alone with Dad when a call comes from the hospital. One of the administrative staff informs me that I need to go back to the hospital and pick up an envelope of my mother's belongings that had been left in security.

At twenty-one, I was not in touch with my feelings, so I responded to this call as I responded to everything else that was happening around me: in a rational, responsible, and intellectual manner. This was my reality. I could touch it, see it, smell it, taste it, and hear it. As far as I knew, these five senses defined all of my actions and perceptions.

At twenty-one, I did not realize that when you are under a great deal of stress, you become more receptive to psychic experiences. The intensity of the stress acts as a catalyst to break down or weaken the barriers of your current reality structure, thereby enabling new perceptions to enter your consciousness.

After making sure my father was comfortably settled, I got in my car and drove ten minutes to Stanford Hospital. I found the room where I was to pick up Mother's possessions and gave the attendant my name. The woman turned out to be a friend of hers, and as she handed me the envelope, she started to express her condolences. I heard nothing that she said, for at that moment, directly in front of me, appeared a vision of my mother's finger with her wedding band on it. There were no words, no voices from above, just the vision. And it wouldn't go away. The lady kept talking and I kept looking at my mother's finger and the ring. Gradually it dawned on me that my mother wanted the wedding band buried with her.

My reality shifted. There was no rational explanation, I just *knew* that this was what she wanted. Once I consciously accepted this, the vision disappeared. I thanked the lady for her kindness and took the envelope to the car, where I opened it. There, among some minor objects, was my mother's wedding band.

Without further thought, I started the car and drove to the mortuary. When I explained to the mortician what I wanted, he thought I was crazy. Here was this twenty-one-year-old kid telling him that he had to open her mother's sealed urn to put a ring in it. He patiently explained that this couldn't be done and I just as patiently explained that he had to do it. It was not an option. Finally, in a tone to appease a bereaved one who has temporarily lost her senses, he agreed, took the ring, and walked back through the door from which he had come. My mother's spirit was at peace.

It is two and a half weeks later. My father's memorial service has just ended and I am standing outside our family's church, Holy Trinity Episcopal Church in Menlo Park, with Bob. John is a ways off talking to friends. Despite the fact that it is the end of March, the day is warm, the sun is out, and blossoms are everywhere. For some reason, probably out of respect for our feelings, people are leaving Bob and me alone.

As we stand in silence, from nowhere yet everywhere comes this overwhelming feeling of divine love. It is as though all the love in the Universe, all of God's love, is shining down upon us and filling our hearts. Then I sense my mother's and father's presence. They are telling me, not in words but in feelings, how concerned they are about leaving us at such a young age. They want us to know how much they love us and that their deep, pure love will be with us forever. As they begin to fade from my awareness, I see their spirits embrace. At last they are together, free of the pain in their bodies and the drive of their egos. For an instant I see them as they truly are: radiant, loving beings of light, no longer defined separately as our mother and father but united as part of our souls. As this magical moment dissolves, an invisible barrier lifts and we are surrounded by friends.

It isn't until ten years later that I mention this experience to Bob. It is one of those rare occasions when we are able to have dinner alone. During a lull in the conversation, I look at Bob and ask: "Do you remember standing with me in front of the church after Dad's memorial service? Did you feel anything special?"

Bob looks back at me and smiles. "Yeah," he says, "our folks were with us. I felt their love."

Since their deaths, whenever people comment to me about how

hard it must have been to lose both parents within a few weeks of each other, a smile comes across my face, and I reply: "No. I felt the beautiful strength and purity of their love and knew that they were happy together. Now when I think of death, I think of this love and the eternal life of the spirit. And I feel joy deep in my soul. It was the most precious gift they could ever have given us."

Looking back, I realize that another interesting experience happened around the time of their deaths. A few days after the memorial service, Bob and I flew our parents' urns to Rhode Island, where our father's family has a plot, for the burial ceremony. After that we drove to New York, where the Dead were starting their 1971 spring tour. I stayed with the band for the New York shows and then flew with them to Boston before returning to San Francisco. On the trip to Boston, I sat next to Jerry Garcia. I felt like being quiet, which gave him the opportunity to expound for the length of the flight on levitation and his ability to float above the ground unaffected by the influence of gravity. Even then, Jerry liked being free from the heaviness of Earth.

It is 1979. I am twenty-nine years old. For the past six years I have been married to David Laing. We are living in a small town called Alamo, about twenty-five miles east of San Francisco. He is president of a savings and loan company that he founded in 1975, and I have been working with him as its marketing director since then. His two sons, Bruce and Dan, often stay with us on weekends, duck hunting or motorcycle riding with their dad, playing with our Irish setters, or joining us at local Grateful Dead shows. I have had no psychic experiences in the eight years since my parents' deaths, so once again I believe that life is "normal."

Then one morning I wake up with the feeling that David is going to die. There has been some stress in our marriage, but nothing to warrant this. He is quite healthy, yet as the days pass I continue to be anxious and worried. For a brief moment I consider telling him, but then I am sure that he will think I'm crazy. What do you say? "Excuse me, dear, but I think you are going to die. I don't know why I feel this way. I don't understand what's happening. I don't even know where this feeling is coming from."

As my fear of his death increases, unresolved issues of my parents' deaths rise up and trigger my fear of abandonment. As much as I would like to handle this alone (a recurring fallacious assumption of mine), I realize that if I don't speak with someone who can help me understand this, I really will go crazy. Now the problem is: How can I get help without letting David know that something out of the ordinary is going on?

"Dave," I say casually one night at dinner, "I'm thinking about taking a University of California Extension course. It's going to be held in San Francisco once a week."

"That's nice," he replies, unsuspecting. "What are you going to take?"

My eyes shift, losing contact with his gaze. "Oh, something that teaches me how to meditate. You know, grounding your energy and stuff like that."

And so begins my psychic training. It takes several years, our separation in 1981, and our divorce in 1983 for me to realize that the death I had foreseen was not David's, it was the death of our marriage. I eventually tell David about my feelings of his "death," and I have to commend him for being less judgmental of me than I was of myself. He never thought I was crazy, although he did think a lot of other things.

It is October 1987. I have just turned thirty-eight years old. Frustrated at having been in banking for the past thirteen years, I am trying to figure out what I want to do for the rest of my life—something that is personally, not just financially, rewarding. I look at my brother Bob and see someone who is successfully "following his bliss," as Joseph Campbell would say. Bob's passion and his profession are one: music. Music is also his means of creative expression. I look at myself. Art is my means of creative expression, but it is neither my passion nor my profession. Maybe, just maybe, though, it is the key.

I contemplate the areas in which I am interested: the environment and children's education. But how do I get from being the vice president of a bank and a financial marketing consultant to being an environmental educator, without having training or background? Not having any other ideas, I decide that the pathway must be through my art; otherwise why would I have been born with this natural talent if it was not meant to be used at some point in my life? Now what do I do?

The idea of writing and illustrating a children's book keeps popping into my mind, but in order to explore that idea, I realize that first I have to begin painting again. The last picture that I painted was after Dave and I separated six years earlier, at a time when I felt my whole life turning inside out. It was an acrylic painting of an old Navajo woman standing very peacefully and solidly in front of a weathered barn wall. She is holding two eagle feathers lightly in her hand, and the deep folds of her warm brown skin give her face a stern yet compassionate expression. The act of painting helped to center and focus me, and it enabled me to express a very deep part of myself—the strong, wise Earth woman—of which I was not conscious. After completing the painting, I was so uncomfortable with the feelings that it touched in me that I put it in storage, where it stayed, hidden away in the dark, for more than ten years. At this point, though, it is still 1987 and I am stuck. I have no motivation to paint.

As it says in the Bible, "Ask and ye shall receive." Let me add the following: (1) Watch what you ask for because you will get it, and (2) Ask for it to be in your highest good and remain open to what happens. I have learned from experience that when I ask for something, I usually get it…along with a lot of other things that I didn't plan on and could do without. The cosmos has a sense of humor, which usually appears during times like this. Gradually, I have learned that it is best, and easiest, to voice intent, ask for it to be in my highest interest, and wait (preferably with patience). I liken this to choosing the river, then jumping in and going with the flow. Having trust and faith are essential elements.

In making a change at this time in my life, I follow the second approach. I ask for help and then wait. Several months later, help comes, but from a totally unexpected source: Bob's dog, Otis. What is even more amazing is that Otis has been dead for almost a year.

Otis was an incredible dog. He looked like a Norwegian elkhound, with a pale gold coat and black markings; however, when he howled under the oak tree at the full moon, he more closely resembled a wolf. He was also very intelligent, highly charismatic, and quite demanding. Once Otis decided that he wanted something, he would not give up until he got it, and once he had it, he wouldn't let go.

It is unclear as to whether Otis found Bob or Bob found Otis. When Otis was two, he used to run freely around Stinson Beach, and since Bob was running freely around Stinson Beach at the same time, it was inevitable that they would meet. Eventually, Bob brought him home.

From my perspective, Bob and Otis were alter egos, and over the sixteen years that they lived together, they absorbed and reflected each other's personality. They were a team, and it is not surprising that when Otis died in January 1987 at the age of eighteen, Bob felt as though his life had been blown apart. It was on the day of the Dead's Chinese New Year show at the Oakland Auditorium, and for the first and only time, Bob arrived over an hour late to start the concert, and during the whole show he never sang one song. He was overwhelmed with feelings of sadness, sick with the finality of loss.

After Otis was cremated, we had a Buddhist-style ceremony and buried his ashes along with a few of his toys beneath a pine tree next to Bob's house. Our lives were indelibly etched with Otis's spirit, but the tree was the only physical reminder of his enduring, restless presence.

As the first anniversary of Otis's death approached, I started to feel pressured. Something was pestering me, but I didn't know what. Then early one Saturday morning as I sat quietly at the kitchen table sipping a cup of tea, I noticed a movement from the side of my vision. I looked in its direction, but nothing was there, so I shifted my focus slightly, and with wagging tail and silly grin, there was Otis. His energy body moved next to me and he nudged my arm with his nose.

Me: "Otis, what are you doing here pestering me?"

Otis: "I want you to paint my picture for Bob. He has nothing to remember me on my first anniversary."

Me: "But Otis, I haven't painted anything since my divorce."

Otis, becoming more persistent: "I want you to paint a picture of me for Bob."

Me: "Otis, you're crazy!"

Otis: "I want you to paint my picture!"

This exchange goes on for days. Finally, as was usually the case, Otis wins. But winning wasn't enough for the old dog. He wants to see the picture completed and presented to Bob before the end of January, only four weeks away. Now I am being motivated to paint not by love, not by passion, but by persistence. Otis does not stop pestering me until I do what he wants, and in an indirect way, Otis has helped me do what I want. He has started me painting again.

In October 1988, just ten months after I finished the painting of Otis, the opportunity to do the children's book arises from the destruction of the rainforest. This might sound strange, but the two are closely related. Having just completed my first workshop with Barbara Brennan out on Long Island, "Hands of Light: Healing Through the Human Energy Field," I take the train into New York City for the Grateful Dead's Rainforest Benefit Concert at Madison Square Garden. By the end of the concert, more than $120,000 has been raised to support rainforest conservation work by Greenpeace, Rainforest Action Network, Cultural Survival, and the Dead's Rex Foundation.

As Bob and I are talking after the show, he looks directly at me and says, "We made a lot of people more aware about the destruction of the rainforest, but we can't stop here. We need to do something more." I feel a click in my head and I look right back at him. "Yes," I reply. "What about doing a children's book with audiocassette tape? We can write the story together, I'll do the illustrations, and you can do the narration and music." Click. "Yeah, that would be great!" Bob replies. "We can reach kids in a positive way, and they can teach their parents. Let's talk about this more when we get home."

Not only did we talk about this when we got home, we did it. The result was the publication of our award-winning children's book with narration and music, *Panther Dream: A Story of the African Rainforest,* in 1991. Using written words, Bob's voice, natural sounds, music, and full-color illustrations, *Panther Dream* teaches children of all learning abilities, teachers, and adults in a positive, creative manner about the beauty and value of the rainforest. Designing the book this way was important to both of us, but especially to Bob, who had been criticized by his teachers when he was in school for being a slow reader and learner. They did not know about or understand dyslexia at that time, and he had suffered greatly as a result. He didn't want any children to suffer as he had.

The need to educate people about our environment in order to preserve it did not stop with the rainforest, and our efforts did not stop with the first book. Early in 1992, Bob and I were at a party talking with some friends about the effect of tropical rainforest destruction on related ecosystems. At that time, few people were aware that the siltation resulting from deforestation was washed into the rivers by rain, and the polluted water was washed out to the sea, where the silt would cover and often suffocate the fragile coral reefs offshore. Like the rainforest, coral reefs support an incredible diversity of life that critically impacts the health of our planet. The foundation that supports much of this life is the reef itself, made up of billions of tiny coral polyps in their limestone bases. The polyps are really animals, not rocks, that need clear water and oxygen (through the process of photosynthesis) to live. When reefs die, all the life dependent on them either dies or moves away, leaving a brightly teeming ecosystem looking like a graveyard. Once again, Bob and I look at each other and feel that familiar click. We both know that this is going to be the theme of our second children's book.

By October of the same year, our bags, scuba gear, cameras, and high-tech digital recording system are packed and we are on our way to Australia to visit the Gumatj people along the coast of northern Arnhem Land and to dive the Great Barrier Reef. Here, we spend a month doing research, taking photographs and video footage, and recording sounds of the coral reefs and the Aboriginal community for use in the creation of *Baru Bay: Australia,* published in 1995. What had once been my vision to write and illustrate children's books was now my reality, and through this process I had also become an environmental educator.

By 1995, my reality was also the world of healing and spirit. I had spent the seven years since my first healing workshop extensively reading and studying about this field. I did additional energetic healing work with Barbara Brennan; psychomotor healing work with Dr. Nicholas Brouw from Amsterdam; shamanic healing work with Jaichima and Vicente, two Huichol Indian shamans in Arizona; angelic healing work with Archangel Gabriel via his channel, Lorna Malmberg, in San Francisco; and psychic healing work with Barbara Courtney in Redwood Shores, California. In addition, I spent as much time as possible alone in Nature, which to me is the greatest healer and teacher of all. From each of these experiences I was able to heal aspects of myself, and I incorporated this knowledge into my own abilities as a healer, both of people and the environment.

In my healing work, I also developed and refined my ability to see and communicate with the realm of spirit, where I could access higher wisdom and guidance. With practice, I became quite adept and confident at channeling this information. I also became comfortable and complacent, and didn't think that anything could surprise me ... until what happened next.

To Lay Me Down

Excerpt from lyrics by Robert Hunter

to Lay me DOWN
ONCE MORE
to Lay me DOWN
WITH MY HEAD
IN SPARKLING CLOVER
Let THE WORLD GO BY
aLL LOST IN DREAMING
to Lay me DOWN
ONE Last tIME
to Lay me DOWN

to BE WITH YOU
ONCE MORE
to BE WITH YOU
WITH OUR BODIES
CLOSE toGETHER
Let THE WORLD GO BY
LIKE CLOUDS a-STREAMING
to Lay me DOWN
ONE Last tIME
to Lay me DOWN

to LIE WITH YOU
ONCE MORE
to LIE WITH YOU
WITH OUR DREAMS
ENTWINED toGETHER
to LIE BESIDE YOU
my LOVE stILL sLEEPING
to teLL sweet LIES
ONE Last tIME.
AND say GOOD-NIGHt

WINGS OF SPIRIT

Transition

tHURSDay, auGust 10, 1995

IT IS SIX-THIRTY A.M., TIME TO CONTACT JERRY'S spirit. The sun is rising as I get out of bed and go to sit in my chair in the living room. The birds are already chattering joyously in the trees outside, their song muffled occasionally by the swish of a car as someone heads to work. I prefer meditating early in the morning when I am still in a quiet, clear state and there are few interruptions. Closing my eyes, I relax my body, raise my energy, and focus within. Memories of the struggle with Jerry the day before drift across my mind as I reach out to him with my thoughts.

Jerry, will you talk with me? I ask. His spirit appears in my vision. It is radiant and peaceful, no longer trying to escape, but there is still no verbal communication.

Jerry, please, can we talk? A vast silence surrounds us.

JERRY! I yell in my mind, hoping to get his attention. Still no response. Why won't he answer?

☯

Wondering what is happening, I raise the frequency of my vibration higher and project my thoughts to Jerry's Oversoul, which resides above the astral plane. The oversoul is an advanced spiritual being that exists in the higher etheric planes in a state of wisdom, love, and truth. It incarnates aspects of itself on Earth, or anywhere it chooses for that matter, in order to grow in understanding and knowledge through the experience of its incarnated body (in this case, Jerry Garcia). The goal is to unify all aspects of itself and return to oneness with All That Is, from which all life evolves. Bob and I had reached out to it the day before, and I hoped that it would connect with me again today.

I focus my energy and ask: *Jerry's Oversoul, can I speak with you?*

Without delay, a deep, formal voice with ageless wisdom replies: *Yes, it is I with whom you are to speak. Jerry's spirit is stuck in the astral and he cannot communicate with you at this time.*

What? I don't understand what's happening, but I do know that the only way I will find out is to continue. Reaching for my paper and pen, I am ready to begin. As I open to receive his communication, fear and doubt suddenly enter my consciousness. I have no idea what he is going to say. Will I be able to stay clear and receive his information without interfering and second-guessing? What happens if I can't do this, if nothing comes to me? I tell myself not to worry. I have done this many times before and am often uneasy at first. Taking a few deep breaths, I relax my body and quiet my mind. With each exhalation, I visualize releasing my fears until I am in a peaceful state. Once again, I open to receive his communication and this time my conversation with Jerry's Oversoul begins.

Wendy Weir (WW): Jerry, are you with me?

Jerry's Oversoul (JO): Yes, I am with you, little sister.

WW: Jerry, why did you choose to transit at this time?

JO: *It was long overdue. I held on because of my desire to be in the physical. To take drugs. To play music. But most of all to be with the ones I loved. We were all together. Sharing the good times and the bad. Sharing the music. Sharing the love. My only regret is the abuse I put my body through. I have problems lowering my vibration sufficiently to take care of my physical vehicle. I have always had this problem. I just haven't gotten it down yet.*

WW: *Jerry, what message would you like to give to people?*

JO: *Just because I have left my physical vehicle to travel in the stars does not mean I have left. Those I love I will always be with. And now that I am free, I can help Bob and others in ways never before possible. I did not choose the name Grateful Dead as a fluke. It has a much deeper meaning, which only now will become evident. This is a time of massive transition. I work best in the stars, free of physicality.*

WW: *What message do you have for the band?*

JO: *My love is with them and my support. There is much left for them to do. As a group, there is a greater message that they need to give to the public right now. Death is not an ending, it is a new beginning. As part of the ongoing now, it is. I still exist, I am not gone. I am here to guide our followers, but from a different position. In this time of transition, they must be shown the path. They must be encouraged to find within themselves the ability to transcend the limitations of the three dimensions which currently exist on Earth and move into the fourth dimension.*

As I write these words, I sense the shift about which he is talking. With my mind's eye, I see a filmy, translucent veil that has been covering the three dimensions of Earth, those physical dimensions that define our existence on Earth in linear space and time, start to draw open, revealing a fourth dimension on a nonphysical plane where feelings, dreams, ideas, and connections to ever higher dimensions exist. As these feelings, dreams, and ideas seek to express themselves in form, they create actions in the third dimension.

Their love for me will help break down the barriers and structures with which they now limit themselves. Have them seek me in the next dimension. I am there. The Earth is now at a point where the physical and spiritual need to be combined and balanced. *I am here to help. Love is the key. Love is all.*

WW: Do you think the band should continue?

JO: No matter what they decide, each individual will carry my love, my energy, my spiritual presence with him. The work can be done as a group or as individuals. But I encourage them strongly to look at the statement they wish to make to the world at this time. It is critical. It will take courage and a deep conviction to step forth into a new reality. I ask each band member to search deeply within his heart, which is the doorway to his soul, to find the answer, the conviction, the passion that will lead him forward in the fulfillment not only of his own life's purpose, but that of the higher purpose for which they all came down here.

WW: Is there anything else you wish to say at this time?

JO: The message is love. Why is it so hard for us to remember this when we enter the heavy physicalness of Earth? There is no time left to play or postpone. The message must be broadcast to all. Those who wish to listen will, and those who do not deny the link to their higher selves and the Universe. I am like the spirit in the folk tale. I am always there to help, to lead, to guide, but first, each person, in his or her heart, must ask for this guidance and help.

A part of my consciousness flashes back in time to 1965 when Jerry came across the term "grateful dead" and wanted to use it as the name for the band. He had been reading *Childe's Ballads,* a book written by musicologist Francis Childe at the turn of the century, in which the theme of the grateful dead is explored in folk tales and ballads from around the world. Of the tales in this genre, a well-known one is "The Traveling Companion" from Hans Christian Andersen's *Fairy Tales.*

In this tale, a kindhearted and loving son sets out on a journey to see the world. He does many good deeds along the way, including paying off a dead man's debt so that the dead man can rest in peace. The son continues on without any possessions or money, having faith that the Lord will look after him. Soon he meets a very wise stranger on the road who asks to join him on his travels. Eventually they come to a kingdom where the son falls deeply in love with a bewitched princess. The son asks the stranger for guidance, and with the stranger's help he is able to remove the evil spell from the princess and marry her. In gratitude, the son asks his traveling companion to stay with them forever.

The traveling companion replies, "No, my time is now up. I have done no more than pay my debt to you. Do you remember the dead man whom the wicked men wanted to hurt? You gave all that you had so that he might have rest in his grave. I am that dead man." [1] And with these words, he disappears.

49

Suddenly it dawns on me. Jerry is now truly "the grateful dead." In passing on, he left some things unfinished. Before he can be at peace, he must complete them. We here on Earth can help. For this he will be grateful and will help us in return.

> *It is time* [JO continues] *to lead the people forth into the next dimension, but many need to be shown the way. Love is the key; it will unlock all doors and light the way. The band can lead the people along this path through their high vibration and I will act as the light in the distance so they have a focus on where to go.*
>
> *You are tiring of the transmission, little one, and it is time for me to go.*

The communication ends. Still in an altered state, I make an effort to look at the clock to see how much time has elapsed. It is seven-thirty A.M. We have been talking for an hour. Even though JO did most of the speaking, he was always aware of the state in which I received his words and proceeded only as fast as my hand could write. Sometimes, if I didn't quite understand a word, I would ask him to stop and clarify it for me. This was important because it is critical for both of us that this information be recorded as accurately as possible.

As I slowly come out of meditation, I allow my mind to wander. Rereading the information, I realize that I feel better about Jerry's death because he has reminded me, not only in words but with feelings, that his love is still with us and that he is still with us, only now in the spirit. The feeling of his unconditional love that had enfolded me during our conversation still remains and I relax into its embrace, trying to eke out a few more moments of bliss before it fades away and I am back in the everyday world.

I look at the clock again. It is eight-ten A.M. Time to get going. I make a mental calculation. Since Bob won't be arriving at the San

Francisco airport until twelve-thirty P.M., I have enough time to get dressed, go to my office, type up the communication, and fax it to his house so that he can read it when he gets home.

Later that afternoon at my office, a friend of mine, Bruce Scotton, calls. He has just talked with Jaichima and Vicente, the two Huichol Indian shamans in Arizona, and Jaichima has some insights about Jerry's death.

Several years earlier, Bruce had introduced them to me when I was getting ready to work on *Baru Bay: Australia.* I was very frustrated at the time because I was living in San Francisco and could not get in contact with the Earth. I felt blocked when I tried to send my energy down to her core, and I knew that I could not write or illustrate the book without being in touch. The book was about a part of her environment, and I needed to feel her guidance and support in order to do the best possible work.

When I talked to Bruce, a transpersonal Jungian psychiatrist, about this problem, he suggested that Jaichima might be able to help. So when she made her next trip to San Francisco, I set up an appointment to see her. Jaichima is a mature yet ageless woman who embodies the child, the youth, the mother, and the crone within the movement of her body and the flash of her eyes. As I walked into the room, I was struck by the appearance of her long, luxurious black hair softly framing her round, smiling face. She was wearing a traditional Huichol blouse with bright, vibrant colors in clashing geometric patterns on white cotton material, a blue floor-length skirt, and beaded Huichol and silver Navajo jewelry. The colors and patterns were riotous, but when I looked at her as a whole, she radiated beauty and elegance.

Throughout our one-hour session, I kept feeling like a young girl sitting respectfully in front of her loving Jewish grandmother, receiving words of wisdom and advice. This was extremely strange because neither of us is Jewish, and Jaichima looks very much the Huichol that she is. Her words were simple and logical, yet I could feel them striking a truth deep inside and shifting my energy in a safe yet unfamiliar way. She was very effective and helped me to remove the block that was hindering my connection to the Earth. Since that time I have worked closely with her and her younger brother, Vicente. The guidance and healing that they have given me over the years has had an incredibly positive influence on my life (to put it mildly), and I greatly respect them, both for their gifts and abilities as shamans and for their unconditional love, integrity, and friendship.

Because of my close relationship with them, I thought that it would be fun to take Jaichima and Vicente to a Grateful Dead concert when the band played Phoenix in March 1994. I asked Bruce, who had been to a lot of Dead shows, and some other friends if they wanted to join us, and they did. Not only was this going to be Jaichima's and Vicente's first Dead concert, it was going to be their first rock and roll concert.

It was Saturday, March 5, a warm and peaceful evening. As the stars were starting to sparkle in the darkening desert sky, I drove up to Jaichima's house. I was a little early in hopes that we could leave on time (my time, not Huichol time) and get to Desert Sky Pavilion to take our seats before the first song. This was my "gig" and I was determined that everything go smoothly. Looking back, I realize that it was foolish of me to think that I had any influence over Jaichima. She has and always will run on her own schedule for her own reasons, and this time was no different. Of course, I'd been checking and rechecking my watch, and by the time she was ready to leave, I knew the show had already started—and we still had a half hour's drive to reach the site. My greatest concern now was that Will Call, the box office window that was holding our tickets, would be closed by the time we arrived and I wouldn't be able to pick them up, along with our backstage passes.

I have never driven so fast down an unfamiliar freeway in an unfamiliar town in my life. I fervently wished that there would be no high-way patrol around to stop me. Fortunately, we arrived at the show without incident and Will Call was still open. As I picked up the tick-ets, I could hear the band finish "Broken Arrow" and move into "Eternity." I knew we were close to the end of the first set, and there was no time to find our seats among the crowd of dancing Deadheads, so I took my friends over to a side rail and we looked down upon the band. They were just beginning their last song.

As I moved to the rhythm of "Bertha," I noticed that Jaichima was looking intently at Jerry. I was about to ask her what she was see-ing with her shamanic vision when the song ended and the band took their break. We were soon surrounded by a mass of people leaving their seats, so I gathered my group together and took them backstage to meet Bob. However, once we arrived in the dressing room area, Jaichima stopped me and asked to see Jerry. When I asked her why, she said that she was very concerned about his health. She told me she had seen him near death, with unfinished business that he needed to resolve within himself before passing on, and it was important that she talk to him.

I tried to contact Jerry, but he had stayed onstage, as he often did, and was totally inaccessible. It was very hard for Jaichima to accept that I couldn't get through to arrange a meeting. No healer sees what she saw without trying to help. I explained to Jaichima that security was extremely tight and that it would be impossible to talk to Jerry in the middle of a show. She felt that Jerry's life was at stake and that it was urgent, but I could do nothing. However, I did promise that I would try again at the end of the show. Unfortunately, this didn't work either, because Jerry left immediately after the encore before I had time to reach him. I even asked Bob to talk to him the next day, which he did, but to no avail.

Now it's a year and a half later and Jerry is dead. On the phone, Bruce starts to tell me what Jaichima had said about Jerry's death.

"Because his exit was not good," she begins, "he would like the music to go on. It is critical that the remaining band members help themselves so that they can let the music come through and finish what he started. He will be there. He will guide them and will channel the music to them. They can now make an end to the bad energy that had been plaguing them on the summer tour."

Jaichima continues, "Jerry is not only offering to help the band to bring forth this music of transformation, he also needs help from the band to bring forth this music to complete his own transition and be free. The name Grateful Dead is very interesting. Jerry is now the grateful dead. He has something he wants from the band members, and he will be incredibly grateful if they help him by bringing the music forth." Even though we were hundreds of miles away from each other, Jaichima and I had come to the same understanding at the same time. In the spirit, Jerry was now *the grateful dead.*

In closing, she says, "The music is needed before the new millennium. We are facing many ecological and political crises that this will help. The fans need this music like a floundering fish needs water. With Jerry's death, a lot of these kids are at a loss and very upset. When he was in a good place in his body, the band was able to bring forth much love between people and contact with the spiritual. The members of the Grateful Dead are an incredible energy for transformation. Jerry's soul can tap them and take them to bigger things."

Jaichima also tells Bruce that she and Vicente are departing today for their land, Ancient Springs, outside of Sedona, where they will perform a fire ceremony and pray for Jerry for seven days. When someone in their tribe dies, the shamans pray for seven days to help the person transition from the physical to the spirit world, and they are treating Jerry as a member of their tribe.

After I get off the phone with Bruce, I type this information up and fax it to Bob.

In the evening, after a private viewing of Jerry's body at the mortuary, some of the band members and close friends get together. Bob mentions these two communications and hands out copies to those who are interested. Everyone's distress and sorrow is great, but this information helps to shed a little light on Jerry's death and eases their pain with understanding.

Saint Stephen

Excerpt from lyrics by Robert Hunter

DID HE DOUBT OR DID HE TRY?
ANSWERS APLENTY IN THE BYE AND BYE
TALK ABOUT YOUR PLENTY, TALK ABOUT YOUR ILLS
ONE MAN GATHERS WHAT ANOTHER MAN SPILLS

SAINT STEPHEN WILL REMAIN
ALL HE'S LOST HE SHALL REGAIN
SEASHORE WASHED IN THE SUDS AND THE foam
BEEN HERE SO LONG HE'S GOT TO CALLING IT HOME

FORTUNE COME A-CRAWLING, CALLIOPE WOMAN
SPINNING THAT CURIOUS SENSE OF YOUR OWN
CAN YOU ANSWER? YES, I CAN
BUT WHAT WOULD BE THE ANSWER TO THE ANSWER MAN?

WILLIAM TELL HAS STRETCHED HIS BOW
TILL IT WON'T STRETCH NO FURTHERMORE
AND/OR IT MAY REQUIRE A CHANGE
THAT HASN'T COME BEFORE

LET THE LIGHT COME THROUGH

Funeral Service

fRIDay, auGust 11, 1995

TODAY IS THE DAY OF JERRY'S FUNERAL. THERE IS NO time to meditate and talk with JO. A friend of mine, Betsy Cohen, has just flown up from Los Angeles and we are trying to get ready for the afternoon service at St. Stephen's Episcopal Church in Belvedere. Tom Paddock, one of the band's sound engineers and computer gurus, picks us up early because we know the church's parking lot will be crowded.

When we arrive, friends and family are quietly milling about in front of the church, exchanging smiles and tears, heartfelt embraces and cherished memories. I see Bob across from the entrance. Our eyes meet. That is enough. Then I see Merl Saunders, Jerry's dear friend and fellow musician, standing alone, lost in pain, tired. I walk over and talk with him, each of us trying to make the other feel better. Soon the front doors of the church are opened. Security is tight as Merl and I leave the brightness of the day and enter the darkness inside.

At the front of the church rests Jerry's open casket. It is

surrounded by arrangements of red and white flowers, one of which resembles a large white lightning bolt on a circle of red. As the small church fills to capacity, I shift my focus and look for Jerry's spirit. I can't imagine that he would miss this event with all of his loved ones, friends, and musicians gathered to celebrate his life. And there he is near his coffin, standing stage left just as he did when he played in the band. On the floor in front of him is a large white floral arrangement filled with roses, and behind him is the dark wood paneling of the church's wall, which accentuates the golden-white light radiating from his core. His shimmering presence is warm and comfortable, reaching out in love and peace to all who enter. A sense of sacredness surrounds us as we quietly take our seats.

The service is led by the Reverend Matthew Fox, the same Episcopal priest who married Jerry and Deborah Koons the previous year. Amidst references to the philosophies of Thomas Aquinas and Martin Heidegger in his eulogy, he refers to Jerry as a "wounded healer."

This is followed by tributes from the band members, friends, and family. Bob walks up and stands in front of the casket. His heart and voice fill with deep emotion as he asks those present to imagine great clouds of joy high in the sky, and to remember all the joy that Jerry brought to so many people. With increasing strength, Bob asks everyone to raise their faces toward the clouds and to reflect that joy right back to Jerry, to give him some of what he gave us.

Robert Hunter, who wrote many of the lyrics for Jerry's songs and was one of his closest friends, follows with his own special tribute.

> JERRY, my friend
> you've done it again,
> even in your silence
> the familiar pressure

comes to bear, demanding
I pull the words from the air
with only this morning
and part of the afternoon
to compose an ode worthy
of one so particular
about every turn of phrase,
demanding it hit home
in a thousand ways
before making it his own,
and this I can't do alone.
now that the singer is gone,
where shall I go for the song?

Hunter's steady, melodic voice continues, but I no longer hear his words. My attention shifts back to Jerry's radiant spirit and I project my thoughts to him.

Jerry, can you talk with me? No answer. Even here, with the energy of so much love focused on him, his spirit doesn't have the ability to respond with words.

Across the aisle, Ken Kesey, author and dearest friend, stands up and starts to speak. My attention is drawn to his powerful face and gentle eyes. His words are strong and clear as he honors Jerry as a "warrior."

"What he did was pry a chink out of the wall and let the light come through that hole. It's up to us," Kesey says, "to keep that hole open. We've got a world to save."

His words, filled with conviction, remind us that the Family still lives, that those people both near and far who feel a part of the Grateful Dead community are still one. We have lost an incredible member, but we, as a whole, are not lost. Within this Family, we have each done something to make the Earth a better place to live, and it is important that we continue. Our purpose remains: love and peace, respect for one another, respect for all of life. This was the message of the 1960s and it is still the message today.

"This guy," Kesey concludes, "is going to kick our ass if we get up there and we haven't carried the torches." With this he takes a lit candle from the head of the pew and raises it up to honor Jerry at the front of the church. Others follow, taking candles, lighting matches and lighters, and holding them up. Soon the church is filled with flickering light and a standing ovation, not only for Jerry, who has left, but for all of us who remain.

After those who wish to speak have spoken, the ceremony closes with the song "My Living Shall Not Be in Vain," performed by several members from Jerry's solo band. Those wanting to say their last good-byes form a line down the center aisle. We move slowly, silently, to the front of the church to view the open casket. Soon I am the one standing beside it. I look down at Jerry's serene face and tears well up in my eyes. His face appears surreal, like a mask from Madame Tussaud's Wax Museum. Everything is properly arranged. His hair is neat and combed. His glasses are resting high on his nose, covering closed eyes. A slight smile creases his lips. I wonder if it is the same smile that they say he had when he died. His body is dressed in his familiar black T-shirt and sweatpants. His hands are gently crossed over his heart, the right hand with its trademark half middle finger carefully hidden by his left, giving him the unlikely appearance of perfection. Without his warm, vibrant spirit animating the flesh, his body seems strange and distant.

Outside the church in the late-afternoon sun, people are talking, sharing, crying, or just standing quietly. As I walk over to Bob, I hear a woman say: "I stayed in the church so that I could say my last good-byes to Jerry alone, and when I looked down at him in the casket, I couldn't believe it." A soft laughter rises in her voice: "Someone in the line had moved Jerry's glasses down on his nose and placed his right hand on top of his left!"

A smile spreads across my face. This is the Jerry we had seen so often: funky and loose, not hiding his imperfections. The cosmos does have a sense of humor, popping up when we least expect it, to remind us not to take ourselves or life or death too seriously.

Stella Blue

Excerpt from lyrics by Robert Hunter

all the years combine
they melt into a dream
a broken angel sings
from a guitar
in the end there's just a song
comes crying like the wind
through all the broken dreams
and vanished years

it all rolls into one
and nothing comes for free
there's nothing you can hold
for very long
and when you hear that song
come crying like the wind
it seems like all this life
was just a dream

KEYS TO THE COSMOS

CHAPTER   6

Keys

SUNDay, auguSt 13—
tuesDay, august 15, 1995

THE DAYS FOLLOWING FRIDAY'S FUNERAL SERVICE ARE
mostly spent with family and close friends at Bob's house nestled
into the tree-covered slope of Mt. Tamalpais in Mill Valley. On
Sunday I join Bob, Natascha Muenter, Rob Wasserman, and John
Barlow to go to the memorial service being held for Jerry at
Golden Gate Park in San Francisco. This is where the Dead played
free concerts for the public during their Haight-Ashbury days of
the late Sixties and early Seventies, and it is quite fitting that the
last show be held here.

It is a beautiful, warm, sunny day, rare for a city with the reputation for fog this time of year. As our car approaches the Polo Field,
we roll down our windows and hear the distant sound of Dead music.
We pass through security at the back entrance and find a parking
space behind the stage. Then we get out of the car and walk up the
slope to the right. At the top, our senses are suddenly overwhelmed
by a sea of bright moving colors and vibrant sounds. Spread out

across the green grass below us are thirty thousand fans gathered from across the country to dance, to listen to Grateful Dead music, to hear the special tributes, but most of all, to honor Jerry Garcia. This is their ceremony. This is their tribute.

Behind and above us, a large colorful painting of Jerry's face graces the backdrop of the stage. Before us, masses of flowers adorn the front. To this, many have added roses, lit candles, and photos of Jerry to create their own intimate shrine. This is their moment, not only to reconnect with friends and reminisce about the good times and the bad, but to say good-bye to the man they love.

Over the next hour, they listen to members of Jerry's family, the band, and several close friends talking about their feelings and memories. At the end, Olatunji, an African drummer who has made many guest appearances with the band, starts beating his drum as he moves offstage. The band members and family follow behind, weaving like a snake in and out of the crowd, playing drums and rattles, singing and clapping. The memorial has become a celebration of life shared by all who are present this day.

With Jerry's death, there has been a major energy shift. The heaviness and problems that had surrounded the band on their summer tour are gone, and the peace and love for which they stood is now shining brightly forth.

On Monday, I return to work without thinking further about contacting Jerry's spirit. I had done what Bob had asked on the day of Jerry's death and, as far as I was concerned, that was it. But in the evening, Bob calls and asks, "Have you talked with Jerry again?"

"No, I haven't talked with him since Thursday," I reply, somewhat surprised at his question. But knowing that he wants to know how Jerry's doing, I tell him, "I'll try in the morning and will let you know what happens."

Awakening to the gray light of dawn and the muffled sound of foghorns, I go and sit in my chair to clear my energies and enter a state of deep meditation. I am still conscious of the early-morning sounds outside, but as I raise my vibration, the sounds fade and I focus on contacting Jerry's Oversoul. However, instead of hearing JO's voice, I see myself entering a maze of dark earthen tunnels. Instantly my mind kicks in and I start to question what is happening. For a brief moment, my fear interrupts the meditation, and then I remind myself that I am safe and ease gently back into the vision.

I travel on a level course further and further into the depths of an immense mountain. There are no lights in the tunnels, although I can see with a type of night vision. Eventually I emerge into a vast stone cavern. Fiery torches are mounted on the walls, casting shadows across the barren dirt floor. Here and there, reflections of light glisten off the moisture seeping from the stone, creating a feeling of dancing stars sparkling in the dusk sky. A warm, white-gold light fills the back of the cavern, beckoning me forward.

As I approach, the light becomes more brilliant and a form takes shape within, seated on a massive granite throne. It appears cloaked in a plain white robe that flows to the floor. The graceful folds of its rough cotton material partially cover two sandaled feet planted firmly on the ground. The loose, spacious sleeves barely reveal two hands resting peacefully on the arms of the throne. Long hair resembling moist green seaweed covers the form's broad shoulders, and its bearded face is hidden in shadow. At first I am confused, because the power and energy of the form reminds me of Neptune. But why would Neptune, mythical ruler beneath the sea, be in an underground cave?

Who are you? I ask. *Why am I here?* There is no answer; then the form shifts from its Neptune nature to an expansive light radiating deep wisdom. All ocean images fade and I wait, trying to determine what to do next.

I would like to speak to Jerry's Oversoul, I continue, trying to sound clear and confident.

A bright light of acknowledgment enfolds me and a voice resonates from around the cavern: *I am here, little one.*

Now I understand the image of Neptune. While in his physical body, Jerry felt most at home scuba diving under the sea, where he could float effortlessly in a world of brilliant sights and soothing solitude. This watery world was a deep, deep part of his essence, and Neptune was the ruler of this world.

We may begin when you are ready, he continues. I pick up my paper and pen and start with my first question.

WW: Bob was asking about Jerry. Do you have any comments about him?

JO: They are well bonded. Bob and Jerry will act as one until such time as Jerry's life plan is fulfilled on the Earth. At that point, they may choose to part or to remain in partnership for future projects in this Earth lifetime.

WW: What comments do you have about the Grateful Dead?

JO: That is such a wonderful name. There are many keys to enlightenment within the gentle folds of its deeper meaning. This meaning needs to be explored and released to group consciousness. How the band proceeds will determine this. I cannot say how, since we on this higher plane cannot interfere with your free will; however, I can encourage each and every one of them to follow their true *feelings, the ones located in the solar plexus region of the human body. Each and every one of them must hold the vision clearly to move forward and spread the Christ/Buddha consciousness on Earth. It is necessary to spread this light as far and as quickly as possible. Music is the key, but each and every band member (and I include each and every one who plays with them) must hold this vision of peace and universal love in order to raise the vibration of Earth and her people and transport them into the next dimension.*

WW: Is there anything else you wish to say?

JO: [Smiling warmly] *Stay in touch.*

The Wheel

Excerpt from lyrics by Robert Hunter

the wheel is turning and you can't slow down
you can't let go and you can't hold on
you can't go back and you can't stand still
if the thunder don't get you, then the lightning will

won't you try just a little bit harder?
couldn't you try just a little bit more?
won't you try just a little bit harder?
couldn't you try just a little bit more?

round, round robin, run around
gotta get back where you belong
little bit harder, just a little bit more
little bit farther than you've gone before

won't you try just a little bit harder?
couldn't you try just a little bit more?
won't you try just a little bit harder?
couldn't you try just a little bit more?

small wheel turn by the fire and rod
big wheel turn by the grace of god
every time that wheel turn 'round
bound to cover just a little more ground

ONE LOVE

Communication

tuesday, august 22, 1995

OVER THE FOLLOWING WEEK I CHECK IN WITH JO, BUT I keep getting the message that I need to take care of the day-to-day stuff and that he will be back in touch. We are working on his time frame, not mine.

During this period I also get thoughts dancing in and out of my head about doing a book with JO. I'm not sure what it is supposed to be, I just feel that a book is "out there" waiting to come in. On the seventh day JO finally reconnects with me during my morning meditation, and the first thing that I ask is for some clarity about these feelings.

WW: Jerry, I keep getting the feeling that I should be writing a book using this information. What are your thoughts?

JO: A tool is needed to communicate with people about death and dying, to help them in the coming transition of our Earth Mother to a higher dimension. The words will act as keys to unlock the deeper knowing that is now closed off to human awareness. I am now a knower. I know what is needed—at least from my perspective—to help other souls deal with the transition from the physical to the spiritual. This means that all will now be shown the path to balance their physical and spiritual selves while here on Earth so that when they die, they will have learned their lessons and will be free of the Earth plane and able to move on into other areas of spirit.

It is critical at this time to move souls out of the astral and physical dimensions of Earth. They are creating a log- jam, and the weight of their unfulfilled consciousness is cre- ating a buildup of great difficulty. To give those now in body on this Earth the tools to bypass this logjam in death and to be free is not only of tremendous universal benefit but also of tremendous benefit for each individual being.

To be truly free to express love is to be one with All That Is. This book can be such a tool. I can work with you to accomplish this objective. I know you are with me, little one.

Believe It or Not

Excerpt from lyrics by Robert Hunter

ONE OR two moments
a piece of your time
is all i am asking
and i'll give you mine
ONE OR two moments
out of all you have got
to show how i love you
believe it or not

i know i'm no angel
my prospects are high
as the flood line in summer
when the river's gone dry
but i'll roll up my shirt-sleeves
and make my best shot
to show how i love you
believe it or not

right now while the sun shines
on the crest of the hill
with breeze in the pines
and a gray whippoorwill
making music together
that guitars never caught
let me show how i love you
believe it or not

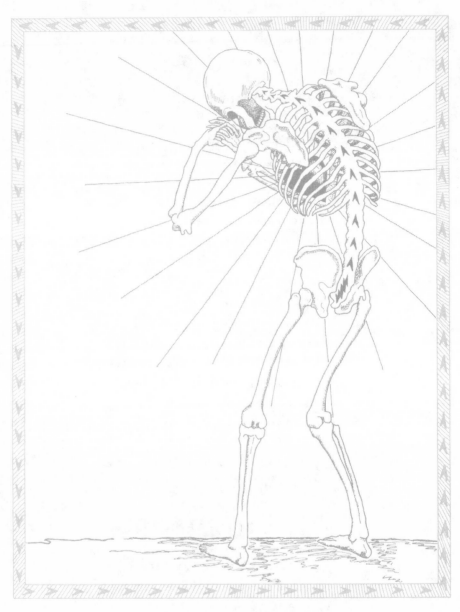

THROUGH THE PAIN

Love

tHURSDay, auGUSt 24, 1995

IT IS THREE THIRTY-FIVE A.M. I AM DREAMING ABOUT writing the book and I am trying to figure out how to proceed. I seem stuck. Part of me feels that I should wake up and start writing this dream down. The other part of me wants to stay in bed and sleep.

Three thirty-nine A.M.: The smoke alarm in my bedroom makes a loud screeching sound and then stops. I am wide awake. Grumbling to myself, I turn on the light, get up, get a chair, undo the smoke alarm cover, and check to see if anything is wrong. It's solid wired to the electricity. I look at my clock to see if the electricity has gone off for a second (which sets the time flashing). Everything is fine. I look back at the wiring. Everything is fine. I put the cover back on, replace the chair, go back to bed, turn off the light, and try to go back to sleep.

A high energy is coursing through my body. Thoughts about how the book can be structured are running through my head. I lie wide awake, determined to go back to sleep. And the more I lie awake, the more upset I get because I begin to realize that spirit is having some fun with me.

"It's four o'clock in the morning, and I am not going to get up and do what you want!" I yell in my mind. "Leave me alone! I want to go back to sleep!" As I'm saying this, I know that it's more to convince me not to listen to spirit than it is to convince spirit that I am not going to listen to it. I also know, from experience, that when spirit speaks, it's in my best interest to pay attention the first time. But sometimes, like tonight, I feel as though my good nature is being pushed a little too far.

Five A.M.: Still wide awake, I give up. I turn on the light, get out of bed, get pen and paper, and get back into bed. Spirit has won. For the next thirty minutes, I write down all the thoughts that come to me.

Five-thirty A.M.: I go out on the porch and watch the crescent sliver of the moon fade as the sun rises to a new day. Beautiful. Quiet. Dawn brings the sound of birds, a noisy blue jay. It's time to get going.

Six-thirty A.M.: I go into the house, sit in meditation, and ask JO if he wants to talk. The response is immediate.

WW: Jerry, are you with me?

JO: Yes, little one.

WW: What message do you wish to give to your fans?

JO: One of love. I cannot say this enough. I didn't do a great job in honoring and maintaining my physical body, but my love was always there. When I was clear, it was able to radiate forth from my heart and my music. When I was messed up on drugs, the darkness and heaviness of my addiction clouded and even hid that love from sight, but it was always there. Now that love can shine forth to all of you. It is unhindered by my physical body. I am free to truly express my higher self, my higher purpose, through your hearts and through my music.

Many of you have felt great pain and grief in my passing. This is a gift I have given you. Through the pain you have been able to search deeply within and release that love that radiates from your true self. You have reaffirmed your sense of self and sense of community. You have found new strength and new (renewed) conviction to help this planet, and this Universe, to reach a higher vibration where love is freely given and received without the devastating fear of harm, guilt, abandonment, ridicule, or manipulation. The love that I have sent to you is only a small fraction of the love that is given from All That Is, the true source of life and creation. This is the light that starts to "enlighten" your darkness and free you of the bondage you have held yourself in. Think on my words. The key is in discovering their meaning within each of you.

WW: What of the music?

JO: The music is the vehicle for this love. Its energy, its vibration, breaks through the subtle barriers of human consciousness to free our inner selves, to give us the opportunity to discover who we truly are. Drugs have been misunderstood and misused. Under proper shamanic guidance and ceremony, they enable one to glimpse more deeply into the sacred. Taken as recreation, for a quick high or to avoid deeper recognition of pain, they become destructive, for they dull our higher senses and block our innate ability to heal ourselves. Our higher consciousness cannot help or even be heard when our energy field is filled with the stagnant black blobs left by drug use. These dark, dead masses of energy bring our vibration down and keep us heavy in the lower frequencies of the physical. I know. I have been there. It is not the way.

WW: What mission do you now have to fulfill?

JO: The same one. I was not able to fulfill it while still in the physical. I had done too much damage to my body to be able to carry the higher frequencies that are now being felt and transmitted onto this Earth. We are in a time of transition. We can move forward with love to a higher frequency, a new dimension. We can go hand in hand with Earth as she frees herself of the darkness, the negative energy that has held her back from her own growth and evolution of consciousness. This negative energy is represented and held here by the actions of man: social injustice, environmental pollution and destruction, greed, fear, control, political manipulation, and much more. This must end. The Earth will be free of it. We have the option to go with her into the light, or to remain back in the darkness. The music is the mission. It will lead all those willing to hear its message forward. But it will not get you there. Only each one of you can do that within yourselves. We offer you a path, but only you can walk it.

WW: What of the band?

JO: The music is brought forth by the band. Each is a highly enlightened soul. The music comes from our spirit, not our physical bodies. We need the bodies to manifest it on this Earth plane, but the music comes from spirit. My spirit will join with theirs, as it always has, in the creation of this music.

WW: Is there anything else you wish to say at this time?

JO: There is much I wish to say, but you have had enough for this session. We will talk again. Go in love, little sister. Go in peace.

As the communication ends, I come out of my meditative state and realize that my hand is feeling cramped from writing so much. We have been keeping a busy pace and I am not used to holding the pen for so long. JO was right. I needed a break.

When Push Comes to Shove

Excerpt from lyrics by Robert Hunter

SHAKING IN THE FOREST, WHAT HAVE YOU TO FEAR?
HERE THERE MAY BE TIGERS TO PUNCH YOU IN THE EAR
BLADES OF STAINLESS STEEL, BATS CARVED OUT OF BRICK,
KNOCK YOU DOWN AND BEAT YOU UP AND GIVE
    YOUR ASS A KICK
WHEN PUSH COMES TO SHOVE, YOU'RE AFRAID OF LOVE

SHAKING IN THE DESERT, WHEREFORE DO YOU CRY?
HERE THERE MAY BE RATTLESNAKES TO PUNCH YOU
    IN THE EYE
SHOTGUNS FULL OF SILVER, BULLETS MADE OF GLASS,
STRING BARBED WIRE AT YOUR FEET AND DO NOT
    LET YOU PASS
WHEN PUSH COMES TO SHOVE, YOU'RE AFRAID OF LOVE

SHAKING IN THE GARDEN, THE FEAR WITHIN YOU GROWS
HERE THERE MAY BE ROSES TO PUNCH YOU IN THE NOSE
TWIST THEIR ARMS AROUND YOU, SLAP YOU TILL YOU CRY
WRAP YOU IN THEIR SWEET PERFUME AND LOVE YOU TILL
    YOU DIE
WHEN PUSH COMES TO SHOVE, YOU'RE AFRAID OF LOVE

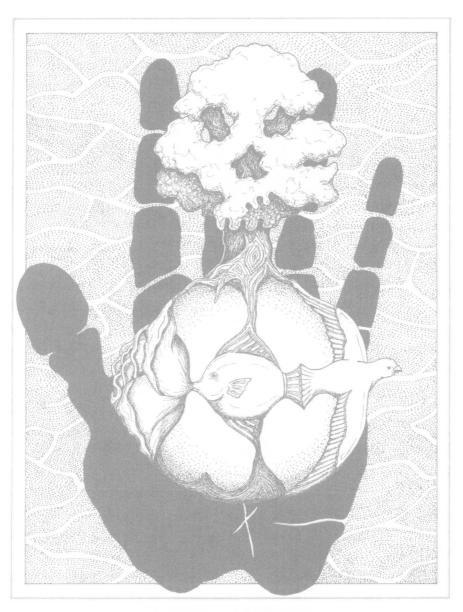

THE FEEL OF NATURE

Nature

fRiDay, auGust 25, 1995

AFTER MEDITATING PEACEFULLY FOR A FEW MINUTES, I connect with Jerry's Oversoul and am surprised to find that he is on a roll this morning. No soft, gentle conversation. He wants to come in, he wants to talk, and he gets right to the point.

WW: All right, dear Jerry, are you with me?

JO: As always, little one.

WW: It feels like you are in a rush to talk to me today. What do you want to discuss?

JO: Nature, or the lack of human understanding of Nature. You never think of the Jerry you all knew in the physical as being highly involved and related to Nature, but he was. When he was under the water, he was home. This was his world. He was one with all around him. The beauty, the vibrancy, the diversity, the peace—all were familiar aspects of his true home in another dimension that he had left to come to the Earth plane. He did not deal well with the physical body while walking on the ground because the concept of weight and the heaviness of the Earth's gravity were very unfamiliar to him. Where he comes from, which is where I—his oversoul—exist, is in a timeless, weightless state where the sounds are colors and take on forms. Each time that he looked at the beauty of life on Earth, he heard and felt so much more than most humans are aware of.

When I hear these words, I remember Jerry talking about scuba diving several years ago. Since 1985, he, Bob, and several other members of the Dead had been going to Hawaii after the New Year's shows to rest and recuperate. Part of the time they would spend diving the beautiful coral reefs off the coast of Kauai and the Big Island. As Jerry once remarked, "Scuba diving satisfies the yearning of going to space; you're in a place where there's no gravity. It kind of takes up the space that drugs left. Night diving is especially magical: The night shift comes out—all the creepers and crabs and lobsters and eels and manta rays tumbling in reverse, backward in loops. You dive every day for a month and it really changes your consciousness." Over a seven-year period, Jerry made more than five hundred dives, and with each dive he felt as though he had entered another world. This was where he felt comfortable. This was where he felt at peace.

JO continues:

Animals, plants, and rocks are not objects or things. They are sentient life. They have purpose. They communicate. They breathe. They have sound and color. They are like mankind, only different. But in this case, different is good, because they do not go around needlessly destroying life in support of their misguided beliefs and need for power and control. All life—except man—exists as one with the Universe. When Jerry saw this life, he felt and heard this oneness. He was a part of it.

I realize that what JO is saying mirrors my own experience and feelings. As a child, I always talked to my stuffed animals, and later to my dogs and horses. "Hi, Mister. Hi, Flip," I would say. "How are you doing today?" Then I would give them a nice pat and continue on my way, not waiting, let alone even thinking, that they might have an answer to my question. I saw them simply as objects that I loved. It wasn't until I started my psychic training in my late twenties that I became aware that they could talk if only I would listen for the answer. At first I had difficulty with this, because not only did I have to completely trust and believe that they could talk with me, but they also had to trust and believe that I wanted to hear their response.

Once I was able to communicate easily with animals, I tried it with rocks, trees, flowers, the moon, the sun, the wind, crystals, my car, my grandmother's ring, and everything in sight. The more I asked and listened, the easier it became for me to hear their thoughts and appreciate their words of wisdom. And the more I heard, the more I realized that we are all connected, that we are all part of the same universal life force, that we are One.

Do not criticize Jerry for his weight, his lack of physical fitness, his inability to deal well with this Earth plane, for you do not see all of the picture. He was more real, more in touch with the true meaning of the Universe, than most of mankind is. He sacrificed much, gave much of himself, to be with you as long as he was.

When you now look at a tree, or a flower, or a fish, or a bird, don't look at it with just your eyes and your mind, putting a preconceived structure and label on it. Look at it from your heart, feel its beauty, feel its sound, feel its communication and wisdom, feel *its purpose and what it might be able to teach you in this moment,* feel *its life. Is it truly a tree, a flower, a fish, or a bird? Ask through your heart and listen for the answer. You might be surprised.*

I silently chuckle to myself as I write down these words: "Is it truly a tree, a flower, a fish, or a bird? . . . listen for the answer. You might be surprised." And surprised I have been, often. For example, I talk with my crystals on a regular basis. The crystal's unique molecular structure enables it to receive, transmit, refract, and reflect light, which is the highest form of energy known in the physical universe. For thousands of years, crystals have been used in ceremony, for meditation, to create a feeling of harmony and peace, for protection from negative energy, for healing, and as a tool of enlightenment. In today's technological society, crystals also have many uses: in ultrasound devices, memory chips in computers, oscillators for controlling radio frequencies in electronic equipment, transducers to transmit energy from one system to another, and condensers to store energy.[1]

For several years, I had been communicating with one of my large, clear quartz crystals and was very familiar with its "voice." Then one day I said good morning to it and a completely different voice, or I should say voices, responded. The entity that had been communicating with me before had been joined by a large group of other entities and they all wanted to talk with me. It was like a conference call. By tuning in to my energy, they were able to get a sense of what it was like to live on Earth: to experience feeling and emotions, the constructs of time and gravity, physical movement, how to breathe, and how to enjoy life. We talked for a while, they gave me some advice from their point of view, and I thanked them and said good-bye. I don't know how long they stayed linked with me, but the next time I talked with my crystal, it once again spoke with its single, familiar voice.

I have also had this experience with animals. I have been speaking with Shammy, my bay quarter horse, for many years. Shammy, an extremely intelligent animal, is boarded at a private home in Woodside, about thirty miles south of San Francisco. The property and surrounding hillsides are covered with pine and redwood trees. I am very used to Shammy's voice and consider our conversations to be part of our regular routine. But one warm summer morning as I was grooming him, I asked if he had any advice or words of wisdom for me, and instead of the usual "Be patient" (I have a very hard time with patience), I heard this strange voice say, "I am the spirit of the redwood trees. It is time. The Earth is shifting to a higher vibration and we are now awakening. The tree people have returned." That was it. I looked up at the tops of the redwood trees swaying in the gentle breeze, then I looked back at Shammy. "Shammy, what happened?" I asked in a startled voice. He swished at several flies with his long black tail, stamped one of his hooves on the ground, and replied casually, "Be patient."

What JO says next is very important.

Be open. Do not limit yourself. Gifts come in many forms. Do not judge them, as you say, by the wrapping. Go deep. Remove the layers that cover the essence of their being and rejoice in what is revealed to you. Look with your heart, see with your feelings, and a new, incredibly rich and wonderful world will be revealed to you. And rejoice, for life is joy, life is love, life is creation. You have the ability to change whenever you want. Look at things differently, with a new perception, and much will shift within you.

Go now and look at Nature with new understanding. She will embrace you, she will teach you, she will give you the key to unlock and release more of who you truly are. Jerry knew this, and he did.

That is all, little one, for now.

All of life is composed of energy, and all energy can communicate. The transmission and reception of thought waves, which are a form of energy, are almost instantaneous, whether you are projecting them to a friend in front of you or to a star in the outer reaches of our galaxy. Some people are able to hold these communications naturally, others require practice. Usually the greatest block that I encounter in helping people communicate with their animals or other objects is their disbelief. Because they believe that anything nonhuman could not possibly talk to them, they automatically close themselves off to hearing the response. Once you change this belief, you open yourself up to an incredible range of possibilities.

If I Had the World to Give

Lyrics by Robert Hunter

if i had the world to give
i'd give it to you—long as you live
would you let it fall
or hold it all in your arms?

if i had a song to sing
i'd sing it to you—long as you live
lullaby—or maybe a plain serenade
wouldn't you laugh, dance, and cry
or be afraid at the trade you made?

i may not have the world to give to you
but maybe i have a tune or two
only if you let me be your world
could i ever give this world to you
could i ever give this world to you

but i will give what love i have to give
i will give what love i have to give
i will give what love i have to give
long as i live

if i had a star to give
i'd give it to you—long as you live
would you have the time
to watch it shine—watch it shine
or ask for the moon and heaven, too?
i'd give it to you

maybe i've got no star to spare
or anything fine or even rare
only if you let me be your world
would i ever give this world to you
could i ever give this world to you

BALANCE

Arrow = Hate   Rose = Love

BALANCED LOVE

CHAPTER 10

Love/Hate

SATURDAY, AUGUST 26— SUNDAY, AUGUST 27, 1995

ON SATURDAY, FOLLOWING WHAT HAS NOW BECOME MY regular morning routine, I sit down in my chair, enter a state of meditation, pick up my pen and paper, and ask JO if he is ready to talk. This morning, however, he says no. He is working on stuff and he'll talk with me tomorrow. End of conversation. I put down my pen and paper, finish my meditation, and spend the rest of the day wondering what "stuff" he is working on.

On Sunday morning, I begin my meditation and immediately feel JO hovering impatiently at the edge of my consciousness, eager to start. He waits until I am ready, and then, for the first time since our communications began, he initiates the contact.

JO: All right, little one, I'm ready to come through.

WW: Is that you, Jerry? You are being very forthright.

JO: I have much to say. We must get going.

WW: Okay.

JO: Today, this morning, we will discuss more fully the aspects of love. We focus, as humans, more on the sexual aspects of love, and sit in wonder about the higher aspects, the ecstatic feelings, of love. It is only natural, in the heaviness of this Earth plane, to be drawn to the lower vibrations as represented in our first, second, and third chakras or energy vortices, but it is not our purpose to stay stuck there.

For those who are unfamiliar with the word *chakra,* it is derived from the Sanskrit word for "wheel of light" and refers to the subtle energy centers located within our physical body.[1] Generally speaking, we have seven major chakra centers, which are located along our spinal axis. The first three relate to our physical experience on Earth. The first one is our root chakra, located near the bottom of the spine. All physical sensations, including our survival needs and instincts, arise from this area. Here we experience the quantity of our physical energy and our will to live in physical reality. It is also through this chakra that our energy is connected to the Earth. The second is our emotional chakra, located in the pubic/sacral area of our body. This is where we process all of our emotions and where we experience both sexual energy and the quality of giving and receiving sexual and physical pleasure. The third chakra is located in the solar plexus area and relates to our mental aspects. Thoughts, opinions, and judgments originate from here and are controlled here. These mental processes also serve to regulate our emotional life and influence our definition of reality.

The fourth is our heart chakra, which bridges the physical dimensions of our first three chakras with the spiritual dimensions of our fifth, sixth, and seventh chakras. It is this center through which we love and feel connected to all of life. It is also the center of our ego drive, which enables us to take action in the physical world. The fifth chakra, located in our throat area, is the center for speech and self-expression. Here is where we take responsibility for our personal needs and desires and experience our sense of self in relation to society. The sixth chakra is commonly referred to as our "third eye." It is located just above our eyes in the center of our forehead. This chakra is the center for both our understanding of mental concepts and our intuition as expressed through clairvoyance, visualization, inspiration, insight, and psychic phenomena. This is also where we physically manifest our creative ideas (from thought, dream, or feeling to physical reality). The seventh, or crown, chakra is located at the top of our head. It relates to our connection with our own spirituality and the integration of our whole being (physical, emotional, mental, and spiritual). Within this center exists our spiritual life, our sense of purpose in this existence, and our place of mergence with All That Is.[2]

Returning to JO:

> *As we grow in knowledge and understanding of our true selves and our connection to our higher self, we need to move this energy up our spine and experience its higher vibrational aspects. Move it through the fourth, or heart, chakra—open up to unconditional love. Move it through the fifth—communicate this love to all. Move it through the sixth—know intuitively that love is all. Move it through the seventh—know that you are love and one with God in this love.*

The vibratory rate of energy in our first chakra starts low and increases in frequency as it rises up our spine, passing through each chakra and out our crown. The more we are able to release emotional blocks and stagnant energy from our auric field, the clearer we become and the greater our ability becomes to safely hold higher and

higher frequencies of energy. Eventually we are able to experience
and express unconditional love, joy, and oneness with all of life.

> *This does not mean that you stop having sex* [JO
> explains]. *It means that you look at the purpose or function
> of sex differently. It is not just for procreation and the ful-
> fillment of sexual desires. It is to be used as a vehicle, with
> one to whom you are deeply committed, to transport you to
> these higher dimensions. Enjoy life! Do not limit yourself or
> close yourself off within structures. Explore, express your-
> self, be creative, be adventurous. Rejoice in all of your feel-
> ings. Do not take yourself too seriously. The Universe and all
> of life has a sense of humor, a sense of joy. Embrace it, for it
> is a part of you that needs to be expressed.*

As amazing as it seems to me, I am just learning about these
higher aspects of love and sexual expression. It took a while for me
to get here because first I had to realize that I had a major block
regarding my sexuality, and then I had to do something about it.
Granted, I grew up in a family with parents who did not openly
express affection. Part of this was due to the era in which I was raised,
when open affection of any sort was not socially acceptable. I remember feeling mortified the summer that I was sixteen when my date
wanted to hold my hand in public, but by fall I was off to the
University of California, where I soon discovered the fun and joy of a
carefree physical relationship.

Much to my surprise and confusion, my sexual attitude changed
after my marriage. As I entered more deeply into a serious commitment, I began to tense up inside with fear whenever we made love.
This lasted for many years, and I didn't understand why until I
started working with my psychic counselor, Barbara Courtney. It was
through her guidance that I was able to uncover the source of this
fear. Although there is no proof, I feel strongly that when I was a

baby, someone, I don't know who, had the intention to molest me sexually. Intent is very powerful, especially when it is directed at someone so vulnerable as a child. I never was physically molested, but the energy of that malevolent intent was so strong that it shattered my open, innocent spirit, and to protect myself I started to fear sexual intimacy. With this understanding came acceptance, with acceptance came release, and with release I became able to reclaim my lost innocence and enjoyment of intimacy.

For the first time, I am also able to grow through joy instead of pain, although pain is still one of my familiar teachers. We are old friends, and change—no matter how good it feels—is not always easy. As Jaichima once told me, we should experience each moment of our lives in an ongoing state of ecstasy. I didn't understand her then, but I do now. This is how I feel, and this is how JO encourages us to live.

> *Now for a different subject: hate. There is no room in our Universe for hate. That is a very low, destructive energy. It means that you do not recognize that aspect of the other within yourself. Others act as mirrors in our lives. If you feel hate, ask yourself why. What part of you needs to be looked at, embraced, and released? Same with anger. When used as a force to motivate you through a personal trial, it is good. When it takes up residence within your being, when you hold on to it, it is not good for you. Look at why it is there in your life, why you are holding on to it. Then embrace and accept the understanding that comes to you and release the anger. Once free in the universe, the anger—which is a form of negative energy—can be transmuted into a more positive energy.*

I actually saw this happen, much to my surprise. It was during a weeklong workshop with Jaichima and Vicente in Sedona, Arizona.

Early one chilly November morning we climbed through the high desert country of Boynton Canyon along a rocky dirt path that snaked between pinyon pines, cactus, and juniper bushes up to the top of Devil's Bridge, a natural rock formation high on the face of a cliff. Once you have reached it, you look out at one of the most breathtaking sights imaginable. In the distance, majestic red mesas and dramatic white rock cliffs jut randomly out from the green tree-covered earth stretching peacefully before me. The vibrant colors of the land are accented by the piercing blue Arizona sky, lying like a soft blanket across the horizon. Here and there a dusting of fluffy clouds appears to rise from the distant cliffs like smoke signals from a ghost fire. Above, the dark form of a hawk circles silently, riding the melody of the wind current that flows gently off the canyon walls, its outstretched wings proclaiming the sacredness of this spot.

The reason we were here was to release our feelings. It did not matter whether these feelings were ones of joy or sorrow, love or hate, reverence or fear. This was the purpose of the site, and different native people had been using it accordingly for centuries. Sometimes this release is done quietly in silent meditation, sometimes it is done with drum or rattle, and sometimes it is done by shouting out across the canyon to the mesas beyond.

When I first came here three years ago, I sat in silent meditation, not because I was at peace with myself but because I was too embarrassed to express my anger or pain openly. I was controlled by my fear of what people would think of me. It didn't matter that there were only twelve of us within a two-mile radius. It didn't matter that we were all here for the same reason. It didn't even matter that to openly express my feelings was encouraged and supported by the whole group. I just couldn't do it. So I sat silently for the first year and the second year. Now it is the third year that I have climbed up to this sacred place and I am determined that I am going to stand on the edge of the bridge, my toes nearly touching the tops of the ponderosa pine trees, and shout out my known and unknown feelings of anger and hurt into the space beyond. I open my mouth and what comes out next surprises me. They are sounds, not words, and their vibration radiates out like ripples in a pond across the quiet depths of the canyon and into the wall of the mesa. As I watch, the sound waves don't bounce off the solid rock as I thought they would; instead, they effortlessly penetrate the cliff face, where their negative energy is absorbed by the Earth and converted into positive energy. This positive energy then flows down to the floor of the canyon, where it enters the roots of nearby trees and vegetation, supplying them with the creative force they need to grow and flourish.

> *If you get stuck in looking at yourself and trying to understand these aspects within you, take some time out to be quiet and alone. With clear intent and meaning, ask to have this understanding revealed to you, then look deeply inside. The answer will come to you, maybe not immediately, but it will come to you when you are ready to hear it.*

It wasn't until several days after my hike to Devil's Bridge that I was able to put names to the sounds that I had shouted. As I sat quietly on a large root of an old, leafless cottonwood tree absorbing the lukewarm rays of the winter sun, I decided to write about my experience. When I reached the part where I shouted sounds out across the canyon, the words *abandonment, rejection,* and *betrayal* flowed unconsciously from my pen onto the paper. I stopped writing and looked at the words. At first I was surprised that such negative feelings could exist inside "such a good little girl," but as I let go of my self-judgment and stepped deeper inside, I could feel their repressed cry rise up from the dark and seek release in the light of day. And so my emotional healing began as once again I released the negative blocks of my feelings into the Earth and felt them converted into positive creative energy, which flowed back up my feet and into my whole body.

Love. Hate. Both are of the same energies, just different expressions of the positive and the negative aspects. Our goal, as sentient beings, is to express a balanced *love, one that does not negate hate but understands that its aspects are a part of all of us and are to be embraced with understanding and acceptance, not acted upon and thrown out at others. Balance is the key here. All that is is a part of us. We must honor and acknowledge it within our being and continually strive to express our higher vibrations in balance with the energies around and within us.*

That is all, little one. We shall return to this subject later.

WW: Jerry, the essence of our communications has shifted. You have become very direct and somewhat forceful in your need to speak. Why the shift?

JO: Little one, the more we work together, the easier it is for us to communicate. We do not need the pleasantries of introduction, so to speak. There is a higher purpose here and one that takes courage to write and speak out about. There is not much time. Those souls that have loved Jerry in the physical and now find him gone from their lives are in pain, both spiritual and physical. It is critical, and I repeat critical, *that the void that has been created be filled with the higher, positive vibrations of love and not the lower, negative vibrations of fear.*

From our perspective, Jerry's passing was a major transition point for the Earth. It is not often that so many people around the planet are so deeply affected at the same time. This is a tremendous opportunity that Jerry has given us in the spirit world and those incarnate on Earth to start moving souls to the higher dimensions en masse *while they are still in the physical.*

Usually people don't start looking at their feelings about death, especially their own, until they are personally confronted with it, either through aging, serious illness, a near-death experience, or the loss of a loved one. And when they do look at death, it is usually on an individual basis. But in the case of Jerry's death, many people were deeply affected by it at the same time and found themselves having to consciously deal not only with the issue of Jerry's mortality but with their own.

The pain of Jerry's death accelerated their need to go within and gave them the opportunity to face their fears now instead of later. In doing so, they could start releasing their own negative energy, thereby freeing themselves of "excess baggage" and allowing their energy vibration to rise higher and higher. Such an energy shift is gradual, happening over a period of time so that the physical body can adjust to this increasing frequency while still staying in balance with the Earth. This is a natural process, once it has started, and should not be forced or controlled.

If you feel pain, sit in meditation and determine that your intent is truly to heal. Make sure that you are not unconsciously sabotaging yourself. If you have a deep commitment to being healed, then clearly express this intention out loud and let it go. Your words will be heard and the opportunity to heal will present itself. However, you must be patient, and once this opportunity appears, you must have the courage to take action.

It is my belief that the more enlightened we become, the more we are able to carry the highest vibration of light and love while still in our physical bodies, and the more free we become to move consciously through life *and* through death. In this state, when our spirit leaves our body, we can choose not to remain in the astral level, trapped by our desire to return in our next life to the pleasures and beauty of Earth. We can choose to move on to higher dimensions and new experiences to enhance our personal growth toward our ultimate reunion with All That Is. Earth is such a beautiful, exciting, physical place to experience the full, intense range of emotions that many spirits do not want to leave. They keep reincarnating over and over again, creating a logjam that stops the natural flow of souls out and on to other realms when their lessons here are done. As we well know, when there is a logjam along part of a river, it affects not only the river but everything around it. According to JO, this logjam of deceased souls needs to be removed in order to bring balance back to the Universe. To do this, he and other spirits are willing to help us "enlighten" ourselves while still in the physical by guiding and encouraging us to release our heavy emotional burdens.

Sometimes we in spirit must disguise things in order to have the truth be revealed. Our motives are always for the higher good, but do not assume they follow a straight path. If mankind cannot learn from good, positive experiences, if he can only learn and grow from feeling pain, then it is pain he will feel. The lesson, the understanding, the inner passage to higher consciousness is the objective. It will happen. It is happening. And we will continue to work within the nature of man—however mankind chooses that to be—to ensure that all on this planet and all in the Universe will have the fullest opportunity to grow in love and return to their source, which is God, All That Is.

My message is urgent. Jerry agreed, before incarnating on Earth, to act as a vehicle for this transition to a higher consciousness. He does not act alone. He acted and still acts with all of the band members. He has, through his death, brought an incredible opportunity for movement into the light. But only by all working together can this movement be accomplished. Listen to the music. The key is in the music. The music will continue. The song, the message, is eternal.

Does this answer your question, little sister?

WW: Yes, I feel better now. Thanks. Go in love, Jer. Go in peace.

Ripple

Excerpt from lyrics by Robert Hunter

IF MY WORDS DID GLOW
WITH THE GOLD OF SUNSHINE
AND MY TUNES WERE PLAYED
ON THE HARP UNSTRUNG
WOULD YOU HEAR MY VOICE
COME THROUGH THE MUSIC
WOULD YOU HOLD IT NEAR
AS IF IT WERE YOUR OWN?

REACH OUT YOUR HAND
IF YOUR CUP BE EMPTY
IF YOUR CUP IS FULL
MAY IT BE AGAIN
LET IT BE KNOWN
THERE IS A FOUNTAIN
THAT WAS NOT MADE
BY THE HANDS OF MEN

THERE IS A ROAD
NO SIMPLE HIGHWAY
BETWEEN THE DAWN
AND THE DARK OF NIGHT
AND IF YOU GO
NO ONE MAY FOLLOW
THAT PATH IS FOR
YOUR STEPS ALONE

RIPPLE IN STILL WATER
WHEN THERE IS NO PEBBLE TOSSED
NOR WIND TO BLOW
YOU WHO CHOOSE
TO LEAD MUST FOLLOW
BUT IF YOU FALL
YOU FALL ALONE
IF YOU SHOULD STAND
THEN WHO'S TO GUIDE YOU?
IF I KNEW THE WAY
I WOULD TAKE YOU HOME

MIRROR OF THE EARTH

Life

mONDay, auGUst 28, 1995

MEDITATE. COMMUNICATE. THERE IS A SENSE OF increasing urgency radiating from Jerry's Oversoul, which is putting pressure on me. We have been communicating almost daily and I am feeling a bit burned out. But I know this information is important and so does spirit. It continues to push me.

Today we begin the session in our regular manner. As soon as I am ready, I ask JO the first question.

WW: Okay, Jer. What's on the schedule for today?

JO: I want to talk.

WW: Let's go.

JO: You have concerns about the ongoingness of life on this planet. Let's address those concerns.

1. *Life is eternal. It does not end.*
2. *Life is energy.*
3. *Energy is eternal.*

What you are concerned about is life as you know it on the Earth plane. That is a very minute aspect of LIFE; however, it is one that is very important to you, since this is the plane and the life upon which your physical experience is based.

As you have recently realized, your true objective as an environmentalist and an artist is not to save the rainforest, the coral reefs, or the mudflats, but to use the environment as a visible vehicle by which to teach people about themselves and to raise their consciousness. Since life is eternal, it cannot die. It can only be transformed. Since energy is eternal, it cannot be lost. It can only be transformed. Life, energy, is constantly changing, evolving, growing.

When you express your concerns about life on this planet, you are expressing your concerns, your fears, about your life on this planet. Will you survive? What state will the Earth be in? Will there still be an Earth?

My mind comes to a shocked halt. In an instant, I see all of the work that I had done for the environment over the past nine years flash before me. The fund-raising events for Rainforest Action Network. The three years that it took to create and publish Bob's and my first children's book and audiocassette tape, *Panther Dream: A Story of the African Rainforest.* The three and a half years that it took to create and publish our second children's book and audiocassette tape, *Baru Bay: Australia.* My speaking engagements at schools and national educational conferences across the country. My cofounding in 1993 of Coral Forest, an environmental nonprofit organization dedicated to the preservation of coral reefs around the world through education and action, and my management of it as executive director.

And, my work with indigenous people in Africa, Honduras, Panama, Australia, and the United States. All this time I thought that I was working to save mankind and the Earth. Now I realize that it wasn't the Earth that needed saving, it wasn't even mankind, it was me. I wasn't afraid for her death, I was afraid for my own. The Earth will survive, but will I?

> *Let me assure you, Earth's time has not yet come to dissolve back into the Universe. Life will continue, but maybe not as you currently know it. In order to ensure the survival of mankind and all life forms in existence on Earth at this time, you must grow in consciousness. The higher your consciousness, the greater your love and respect, first of all for self, then for others. You must always heal yourself first before you can truly heal another.*

This is a very hard lesson to learn: healing oneself first. It was so easy and natural for me to focus on taking care of others, on helping them to heal spiritually, emotionally, and physically, that I (quite conveniently) had little time left to focus on me. It was on another trip to Sedona that the importance of my need to start healing myself became clear.

The dark, rain-filled clouds of a desert storm were drifting in over the mesas and blocking the bright sun when, on an impulse, I decided to drive out to see the prehistoric pictographs outside of town. As I approached the parking area, a fierce torrential downpour started. I stopped the car, turned off the engine, and stared up through the water streaming down the windshield at the caves in the cliff where the paintings were located. When the last of the rain-soaked tourists had driven away, I got out of my car and splattered through the sticky red clay mud up the path to the first cave. I stayed there briefly, gazing at the primitive, powerful drawings, but whatever had drawn me to this spot was not there.

Walking back out into the rain, I turned left down an inconspic-
uous side path now covered by a narrow stream of water. This path
led to a much smaller cave that was decorated not by figures but by
the blackened smoke of ceremonial fires over hundreds, maybe even
thousands, of years. It was dry inside, so I sat down on the earth and
leaned my back against the cold red-rock wall. Closing my eyes, I listened peacefully to the staccato of the rain outside. The stress and
tension eased from my body and slowly a vision appeared in my
mind's eye. It was the rock wall behind me, animated into the form of
the Earth Mother cradling a human baby gently in her cragged stone
arms. Then I became that baby and could feel the heat of all the fires
warm my body, and the Earth Mother cooed softly in my ear: "You
must heal yourself first before you can heal me. In healing yourself,
you heal me."

> *Look at your efforts as a reflection of your fears. Then
> look at your fears. Where do they come from? Why are they
> here? Go deep within to find the answer. You know that past
> lives of which we will not speak have influenced the creation
> of those fears, but that is the past. This is the present. Learn
> from your past experience, and transform that negative
> energy of fear, which holds the frequency of your vibration
> down, into the energy of love, which can grow and expand
> and help to heal others.*

"Past lives of which we will not speak," JO says. He has no need
to speak of them. When I hear these words, fear rises up and images
of burning at the stake, being ravaged and beaten by invaders, muti-
lated and killed in battle, abandoned in a wet, infinitely dark dungeon, pass across my inner vision. I was a healer and midwife. I was
a country wife. I was an idealistic young man going to war to defend
his homeland. I was an honorable statesman who held true to his
beliefs. As these visions fade, more appear. A sense of other lives and

pain dances in the background of my mind like silent actors on a screen. In many lifetimes I suffered. Whether I had been good or bad did not matter, and the memory of this pain and horror and shock settled deep within my bones and tissue, into the very cells that compose my present body.

"…but that is the past. This is the present," JO says. But my fears are real. I feel them now. And because I feel them in the present, I can release them in the present and be free of the negative influence they have over my life. The present is where our power resides. I choose love, I choose freedom, and in making this choice I start the process of healing the shattered parts of my being, releasing the traumas of past, yet present, lives and becoming whole once more.

The Earth acts as our mirror, as we do the Earth's. The Earth has allowed circumstances to get to this point because she, too, had something to learn. Now that she is accomplishing this, she is ready to let go of the fear and negativity that has existed on her, as a parasite exists on and feeds off of another living object. She is ready to release the darkness and move to a higher frequency of light.

Do not think of the Earth as an inanimate ball of rock and dirt moving through space. She is a living, breathing, growing, evolving, sentient being. The first humans knew this and honored her with ceremony and respect. All indigenous cultures know this and honor her spirit to this day. Only the industrialized societies, where science and organized religions dominate humankind's view of the world, have forgotten. But this, too, is starting to change as we grow and change. The spirit of the Earth is referred to, once again, as "Gaia," the ancient Greek goddess of the Earth. Along with this comes the image of a female, maternal spirit that can be both loving and angry, creative and destructive, healing and harmful. She is not stagnant but alive, and she gives life to all that grows on her. And as life grows and evolves on her, she grows and evolves. As our path moves toward the light, her path moves toward the light. However, she can get there without the existence of humans on the Earth. We, on the other hand, cannot get there without her.

Look back upon your feelings and experiences when Jerry died. When you first checked on him, his soul and spirit were in a state of radiant ecstasy. He was euphoric to be free of the negative weight of his body. Then he went to a place where you and Bob had to go talk to him. You both knew that for Jerry to learn the lessons he needed to here on Earth and to fulfill his life's plan, he couldn't exit stage left. He had to return to the physical plane in spirit to continue his work. You talked to him, worked with him, and brought him back. Although he knew this was necessary, he was not very pleased, but he is here in acceptance, humor, and love to ful-fill his commitments.

The point in all of this is, as Jerry shed the negativity and darkness that existed and was represented within his physi-cal body, so the Earth will shed the negativity and darkness that is represented on her physical body. Like Jerry, she will free herself and move to a higher frequency of light. However, unlike Jerry, she will not have to be brought back. She will shift her frequencies to a higher vibration while still in the physical and will bring all life that is able to meet that vibration with her. The rest, the negative aspects, will be transformed to a different dimension, where they will have the opportunity to continue working on their spiritual growth.

Will they die? As you see it in the physical, yes—many will. Will they die in the spiritual sense? No. Do not allow your fears of loss in the physical to absorb your being. It is a fear of death, on a very deep level, that needs to be released.

*If you fight to preserve life, then you fight to preserve your
own life. That is the root of the issue. If you fear the loss of
life, you fear the loss of your own life.*

*Shift your focus, keep up the fight, for any and all efforts
to raise people's consciousness are vital. But shift your energies from fear to love. With the energy of love, there is freedom. With the energy of love, there is total acceptance. With
the energy of love, there is honoring of the other and knowing that whatever path the other takes is the right path for
them. Be clear. The work you do is for your own growth to a
higher level of consciousness. You set the frequency, which
will then be broadcast out to others and help to raise their
frequencies and awareness.*

*I have used you, little one, as an example. I hope you do
not mind, but there is much that others can learn from your
feelings and experiences.*

No, I do not mind. I am uncomfortable with the feelings and
fears that have arisen, but I know that JO has said this not only to
help others but to help me.

*Go now. You need rest, although I know you will not
take it. Find time to be alone, to go within, to listen to the
sounds, the music, in the depths of your soul. There you will
find what you seek.*

WW: *Thanks, Jerry. I will, but you are right—it won't be
today. Take care.*

JO: *We will talk again tomorrow.*

☯

As I finish typing the conversation, I start to smile. Are we having fun yet? I had no idea that in bringing forth this information, it would also bring forth some of my own inner issues. I honestly didn't think that I had a fear of death, but the deeper I go within, the more I sense its presence in the darkness. Why are we so devoted to preserving life, if the preservation of our own life is not at the root of it? JO brings up some interesting issues, not all of them comfortable.

A thought suddenly occurs to me. Bob and I worked to bring Jerry's spirit back so he could complete his mission on Earth. Is this his humor coming out via JO? I can just hear Jerry saying with a radiant grin, "If I have to come back and deal with this stuff, so do you!"

Broke-Down Palace

Excerpt from lyrics by Robert Hunter

fare you well, my honey
fare you well, my only true one
all the birds that were singing
have flown except you alone

going to leave this broke-down palace
on my hands and my knees i will roll, roll, roll
make myself a bed by the waterside
in my time—in my time—i will roll, roll, roll

in a bed, in a bed
by the waterside i will lay my head
listen to the river sing sweet songs
to rock my soul

river gonna take me
sing me sweet and sleepy
sing me sweet and sleepy
all the way back home
it's a far-gone lullaby
sung many years ago
mama, mama, many worlds i've come
since i first left home

fare you well, fare you well
i love you more than words can tell
listen to the river sing sweet songs
to rock my soul

MUSIC OF THE UNIVERSE

Music

tuesDay, auGust 29, 1995

JERRY'S SPIRIT WANTS TO COME IN THE MOMENT I SIT down to meditate, but I am not ready yet and ask him to wait. While I clear and raise the frequency of my vibration, I feel him constantly pushing me to begin. His impatience disrupts my meditation and I open the communication a bit irritably.

WW: Okay, Jer.

JO: I've been waiting.

WW: I know.

JO: Today's discussion will be very different than before. It will be one of modalities. Since you have no musical background or training, it will be hard for you to grasp what I am saying, but after your studies you will understand.

Studies? Last Saturday I visited the Rosicrucian Egyptian Museum in San Jose and afterward I walked into their bookstore to browse. I was somewhat surprised to find myself in the music section, staring at the book *The World Is Sound: Nada Brahma* by Joachim-Ernst Berendt.[1] I enjoy music, but I know nothing about it except what I learned from an obligatory year of piano lessons when I was eight. Almost all of this has long since been forgotten. Then I noticed the subtitle, *Music and the Landscape of Consciousness.* For some reason, I decided it would be interesting to read, and so I bought it.

Over the past week, I have covered only the first seventy pages. I read some before going to bed each night, but when I reached the technical part, I stopped because I kept falling asleep and forgetting what I had just read. However, despite my lack of memory retention, this book must be the "studies" to which JO refers. Now this leads me to wonder: If JO is having an unconscious influence on me by guiding me to this book before our session, am I having an influence on him? The channel or link between us goes both ways.

With little comprehension, I continue to write what JO is saying.

> *Modalities are actually rhythms or waves of energies that change in frequencies and modulate to one another and to the Universe at large. Tone, sound, music, all are influenced by what is going on around them on the basis of energy. Sometimes a band is on and is magic, other times it is not. This is due in part to the outside influences brought to bear on the purity of the modalities.*
>
> *As the modalities are influenced by the energies around them, so is mankind. No one stands alone. All influence one another. The vibrations and modalities of man are sent out to the Universe; they are transmitted. Others send out theirs. It is an ongoing exchange, transmission and reception, of energies linked by avenues or channels or filaments, that transports these energies.*

*If you wish to shift modalities, either in the music you
play or the frequency you transmit, you must shift your own
energies first. These are the primary energies, since they originate from you, which influence the secondary energies,
which are all those that surround you.*

*To shift your vibration upward, you must be clear within
so that the energy has the "space" to resonate at a higher
pitch. The clearer you become within, the higher your pitch
or signal (or signature) and the purer the harmonies and
interrelationship of the modalities.*

*I know this does not make much sense to you, but I am
preparing you for further, more in-depth discussions of the
true value and purpose of music. After you have done your
studies, we will continue with this conversation.*

That is all, little one. I will see you tomorrow.

JO is right. I don't understand a thing. So not even thinking about the
book I just bought, I decide to look up the definition of *modality* in
the *Random House Dictionary of the English Language,* which defines
the following:

> *Modality*—1. the quality or state of being modal.

> *Modal*—2. Music: a. pertaining to mode, as distin-
> guished from key; b. based on a scale other than
> major or minor.

> *Mode*—5. Music: any of various arrangements of
> the diatonic tones of an octave, differing from one
> another in the order of the whole steps and half
> steps; scale.

> *Diatonic*—1. noting a scale that contains five
> whole tones and two semitones, as the major,

minor, and certain modal scales. 2. of or pertain-
ing to the tones, intervals, or harmonies of such
a scale.

The dictionary has been of no help. I still don't understand!

It has now been over two years since I wrote the above. As I begin to
edit and rewrite the chapter, the thought occurs to me that I should
look up *modality* in the index of the book that JO wanted me
to study, *The World Is Sound: Nada Brahma.* Why didn't I think
of this before? I take the book off the shelf where I keep my reference material and I open to the index, where I immediately find the
word *modality* with page 203 listed after it (this was definitely not in
the first seventy pages that I had read!). I turn to the page and begin
a fascinating and fully comprehensible journey into the world as
sound.

"After you have done your studies, we will continue with this
conversation," JO had said two years ago. I never completed my studies and JO never continued the conversation—that is, until today.
Now I understand the message that JO wants to give. Even though I
am not channeling this information, he is speaking to me through
impulses and guiding me in my reading.

According to Joachim-Ernst Berendt, in the mid-1950s through
the 1960s, a new musical-spiritual consciousness developed in
the United States, led by the music of John Coltrane, the well-
known jazz musician, tenor, and soprano saxophonist who died in
1967. His influence permeated the rock and pop music of that era
and the consciousness of the young people who heard it. Jerry
Garcia, Bob Weir, Phil Lesh, Pigpen, Bill Kreutzmann, and Mickey
Hart, all members of the Grateful Dead, were among those young
people.

This music had roots both in the East and the West, and it differed from traditional European music by the fact that it was *modal.* This means that "it is based not on continually changing chord structures like our occidental music, but on a scale, a *mode,* or a single chord.... Modal music has to do with a certain mental, spiritual attitude."[2] Thomas Moore explains it a little more simply, using chant as an example. "Chant is modal. It doesn't have the drive toward ending or the insistent relationships between notes and chords that modern music has...."[3]

Today, thousands of rock and pop groups all over the world play modally, in large part due to the influence of John Coltrane. His jazz was influenced by the improvisation principle of the East Indian ragas, and his deep spirituality was expressed by his music technique, his modality and sound. Coltrane's influence can be seen in the sound of the Grateful Dead, who are famous (and at times infamous) for their musical improvisations and their ability to use sounds and scales to produce emotional feelings. The Dead, in live concert, were able to lead their audience on a brilliant, spontaneous journey through the uncharted lands of a new consciousness.

This musical and spiritual consciousness is best expressed in the following excerpt from a text by the great Sufi master, Hazrat Inayat Khan.

> What we call music in our everyday language is only a miniature from that music or harmony of the whole Universe which is working behind everything, and which is the source and origin of nature. It is because of this that the wise of all ages have considered music to be a sacred art. For in music the seer can see the picture of the whole universe....
>
> All the religions have taught us that the origin of the whole Universe is sound. No doubt, the way

in which this word is used in our everyday language is a limitation of that sound which is suggested by the scriptures.

The music of the Universe is the background of the small picture which we call music. Our sense of music, our attraction to music, shows that there is music in the depth of our being. Music is not only life's greatest object, but it is life itself.

When one looks at the cosmos, the movements of the stars and planets, the law of vibration and rhythm, all perfect and unchanging, it shows that the cosmic system is working by the law of music, the law of harmony; and whenever that harmony in the cosmic system is lacking in any way, then in proportion disaster comes to the world, and its influence is seen in the many destructive forces which are manifest there. The whole of astrological law and the science of magic and mysticism behind it are based upon music. Therefore the whole life of the most illuminated souls who lived in this world, like the greatest prophets of India, has been music. From the miniature music, which we understand, they expanded the whole Universe of music, and in that way they were able to inspire.

Every person is music, perpetual music, continually going on day and night; and your intuitive faculty can hear that music. That is the reason why one person is repellent and the other attracts you. It is the music he expresses; his whole atmosphere is charged with it.[4]

In reading these words, I feel they express the essence of what JO wanted to say about "the true value and purpose of music." At last I am able to comprehend, on a deeper level, the meaning of music, its creative primal force, and its relationship to the Universe and the divine, both within us and without.

Black Peter

Excerpt from lyrics by Robert Hunter

aLL of my fRiends come to see me Last niGht
i was LayinG in my Bed and DyinG
annie Beauneu fRom saint anGeL
say, "the weatheR Down heRe so fine"

Just then the wind
came squaLLinG thRouGh the dooR
But who can
the weatheR commanD?
Just want to have
a LittLe peace to Die
and a fRiend oR two
i Love at hanD

see heRe how eveRythinG
LeaD up to this Day
and it's Just Like
any otheR Day
that's eveR Been
sun GoinG up
and then the
sun it GoinG Down
shine thRouGh my winDow anD
my fRiends they come aRounD
come aRounD
come aRounD

FLIGHT OF JOY

CHAPTER 13

Joy and Healing

WEDNESDAY, AUGUST 30, 1995

As I sit down in my chair to begin meditating, I hear the birds chirping and singing happily outside, heralding the dawn. In contrast, JO is not happy. In fact, he feels quite irritated. I can already sense his presence hovering above me, pushing anxiously to begin.

I am surprised that, at the high level of the oversoul, I would be picking up on this kind of less-than-perfect behavior. For some reason, I always pictured the oversoul as existing in an eternal state of bliss, like the images of resplendent angels in a Raphael or Leonardo da Vinci painting. But as soon as I complete this thought, another one appears: Since the God/Goddess Force or All That Is is composed of all aspects of existence, including what we might term negative emotions, it only stands to reason that our oversoul and our own selves that are a part of All That Is would also contain and express these feelings.

This understanding puts my mind at ease and I begin my

meditation. JO, however, is still pressuring me to open the link, and soon I am starting to feel irritated, too.

WW: Not yet.

Return to meditation. Two minutes later.

JO: Little one, are you ready?

WW: Not yet.

Return to meditation. One minute later.

JO: I have much to say!

WW: Not yet!

Thirty seconds later. I give up. How did he get to be so pushy? I pick up pad and pen, and say…

WW: Okay, Jer. Let's roll.

JO: Thank you. I know I am impatient, but from my perspective there is much to say and not a lot of time to say it in. Please understand.

WW: I do, but remember, on any level, patience is a virtue.

JO: [Smiling] Yes, unfortunately, that has never been one of my virtues!
Today we will discuss something you are much more familiar and comfortable with: joy. Joy is an incredible energy when allowed to express itself in all of its radiance

and purity. It is one of the strongest energies used in healing and it comes from within. Joy is generated from the soul level and is expressed through the feelings of the heart. It shines from within and goes out, affecting positively all those within your energy field.

Have you ever noticed that a hearty laugh and a warm smile make you feel better?

When someone enters into this field, your frequency of joy triggers a like response within them. They in turn (if all is well) raise their frequency to match yours as best as possible and start to generate joy within themselves. Joy is contagious. Humans like to feel good, feel joyful.

As I said, joy is one of the greatest healers, for it raises your vibration and this higher vibration breaks loose the negative energy and blocks that exist at a lower vibration so that they become free to rise up and be released. I realize that when one is in pain it is hard to express joy, but it is very important for one in pain—either physical, emotional, or spiritual—to be around people who are joyful and happy. The energy of the one in pain will try to automatically match the vibration of those in joy, and this process will aid the healing. You should never be negative, sad, or in fear when you are with someone who needs healing. It only makes things more difficult for them. Be in joy. Be in love.

Many books and articles have been written about the healing powers of love and joy. Case after case has been scientifically documented about patients who have healed faster because they are in a loving, happy environment versus an unhappy, stressful one. Sandra Levy, associate professor of psychiatry and medicine at the University of Pittsburgh, wrote in the mid-1980s that her studies of women with breast cancer showed that the second most significant factor in the survival of her patients was a sense of joy (the first was the length of time of the disease-free interval between diagnosis and recurrence).[1] Dr. Bernie Siegel, author of the bestselling books *Love, Medicine and Miracles* and *Peace, Love, and Healing,* supports Dr. Levy's findings about joy, adding that disease has the power to teach us this lesson. He writes, "The healing mechanisms are the same for all diseases and for all patients as well as their doctors. We must all confront the reality that no one lives forever. Illness and death are not signs of failure; what is a failure is not living. Our goal is learning to live—joyously and lovingly. Disease can often teach us to do that."[2]

> *This also applies to the dying process. If you are in fear, in any way, this fear will be felt by the other who is dying. In the dying process, people are trying to raise their frequency higher and higher so that they are no longer held back by the lower frequencies of their Earth body and they can be free to transition into spirit. If you are in fear, if you are in sadness, if you are in emotional pain, this will make their dying process more difficult. If you truly love them, then show them this love.*
>
> *Detach from your own issues—they are* your *issues—and be with the other with joy and love, supporting them to the best of your abilities in* their *process. This, in turn, will help you deal with yours. The dying process can be a very healing process for all concerned, but you must be there for the other, not for yourself. In your society at this time, the dying process is very misunderstood. It should be a time of celebration, of rejoicing. It should not be one of sadness and mourning.*

When my parents died, I was twenty-one years old. I had no experience with a loved one dying, or anyone dying for that matter, so I purchased and read the book *On Death and Dying* by Elisabeth

Kübler-Ross, M.D., to help me understand this process. The information was very helpful on an intellectual level, but it could not prepare me to deal with my emotions. Because I didn't have the maturity or the skills to experience these emotions (I was still working with the old belief "You have to be in control, so it's not okay to cry"), I was never able to acknowledge and integrate the pain of their passing. My whole being was focused on getting through as best I could, which meant being responsible, efficient, strong, and positive. In order to do this, I unconsciously buried my hurt and fears deep inside, closed the door, and threw away the key. I was there for my mother with love and positive support, both while she was conscious and while she was in a coma. She died. I was there for my father with love and positive support. He died. I was there for our friends during the ensuing phone calls and memorial services. And I was there for Bob and John, as they were for me. At last, I thought that this whole dying process was over, and it was—for my parents, not for me.

JO says that "the dying process can be a very healing process for all concerned." This is very true. Time is irrelevant. My emotional healing started with the death of my marriage ten years later. One type of death triggered memories of the other. With professional counseling, the key was found, the door opened, and all the emotions that had been deeply buried started to rise like ghosts from a graveyard in a bad horror movie. I became aware of my fears of abandonment and loss of love, and with tears streaming down my face, I finally acknowledged the immense pain that I had felt with my parents' deaths. At the end of two years, I finished my counseling sessions feeling well healed.

Time is irrelevant. Twenty-six years later I have once again been faced with unresolved emotional issues regarding my parents' deaths. This time, they are VERY deep. Now I understand what JO meant when he said, "…be with the other with joy and love, supporting them to the best of your abilities in *their* process. This, in turn, will help you deal with yours."

On August 2, 1997, Bob and his band, Ratdog, were playing at the Further Festival at the Shoreline Amphitheater in Mountain View, approximately forty miles south of San Francisco. It was a home gig, so he invited his birth father, Jack Parber, and his family and his birth mother, Phyllis Critchfield, and her family. Bob was adopted at birth, but over the past two years he has successfully and happily made contact with his birth parents, both of whom live in the area. Phyllis and two of her sons, John and Stewart, arrived late, so it wasn't until Bob was about to go onstage that we learned that Phyllis had just been diagnosed with an inoperable brain tumor and had only a short period of time to live. After the show, I asked Phyllis if I could visit her in the coming weeks to be with her through the dying process. She gave me a knowing smile and agreed.

I spent many days during the month of August driving an hour to her home in Fairfield to sit and talk and laugh with her, or just to hold her hands with love. After the first two weeks, it dawned on me that the roles were being reversed. I still did the driving, but Phyllis was sitting and talking and laughing with me, or just holding my hands with love as memories of my own mother's death welled up inside of me, crying to be released. My intention was to be there for Phyllis as I wish I had been for my mother, with the love and wisdom that only experience and emotional maturity can bring. And in being there for Phyllis, I triggered the painful memories of my own mother's death, and in Phyllis's presence I was able to look at them, feel them, and finally heal them.

In Jerry's passing, those of his Family knew the truth of this [that death is a time for rejoicing] *and celebrated both his life here on Earth and his life in the spirit. All knew that life is eternal and all embraced him with joy on his journey. The pain that each one felt was real, but it was not a pain for Jerry. He was free. It was a pain for each individual because it brought up fears and issues within each one that needed to be healed.* **This is a gift.** *This is part of the incredible power to heal ourselves, if only we recognize it as such. I did not say the process is fun, but it allows each individual the opportunity to look at new aspects of her/himself and to heal them.*

Phyllis died peacefully on the afternoon of September 2, and with her passing the deep pain of my parents' death passed, too. At times I still cry when I think of the death of my parents and Phyllis, but now my tears are full of love, not pain, and my heart is open with joy, not closed with sorrow.

Joy. Joy is love. Joy is peace. Joy is within each and every one of us if only we listen to it calling, follow its song, and open the doors to where we so often keep it hidden behind pressure, guilt, work, obligations, fear, and pain. Allow the light of joy to shine forth from within, allow it to penetrate the Universe, and you will be transformed, for life within you will be raised to a higher vibration and the life without you will respond to this shift.

As Bob said at Jerry's funeral and memorial services: Shine your joy back to Jerry. Give him back something of what he gave you. This is a lesson we should incorporate into all of our lives, every day. Open up, allow your joy to shine forth, and feel the radiance, the joy, shining back to you.

That is all, little one. How do you feel?

WW: Actually, Jer, I feel joyful. Thank you. This was a wonderful gift. Go in joy, dear one.

JO: We will talk again soon.

The next day I leave for a business trip back East and am out of town from August 31 to September 6. One night when I am alone in my hotel room and unable to sleep due to the three-hour time-zone change, I decide to communicate with JO, if possible. The reason I say "if possible" is that when I meditate, I must be in a place where I feel protected on an energetic level and can safely open the link to channel. There is a danger in channeling energy at the high frequency that I use, because the strength and brightness of my transmission can attract not-so-well-intentioned spirits that might want to harm me. This sounds like a science fiction story, but it's not. It's my experience.

When I first started communicating with spirit, I was thirty-six years old. I had been seeing nonphysical images and beings since I was twenty-one and understood what was being communicated based upon my feelings, but I couldn't have a two-way conversation. Finally one day I decided that it was time I learned how to channel. I went to a bookstore, bought a book on the subject, and read it thoroughly.[3] Then I sat down in my chair to meditate, raise my vibration, try to remember everything I had read, and open the link. It worked! I reached spirits on a higher level. This didn't surprise me, because I expected it; however, I did not expect to discover that not all spirits are nice and friendly. I quickly learned that if you don't raise your frequency high enough to get out of the lower astral planes, you can tune into some pretty mean, trashy fellows who do not have your best interests at heart.

This only happened to me once. It only needed to happen once. I was expecting angels, and instead I opened the channel to a bunch of barbarians and pirates with knives, cutlasses, and all sorts of death-wielding instruments. It was like standing in an elevator when the doors open on an unknown floor and you look out at all these strange faces staring back at you, frozen briefly in time. Just as I saw them, they saw me, a look of astonishment swept over their faces, then they decided to attack. I was frozen with shock. Could they actually kill me in the spirit? My mind told me no, it didn't think so, but it wasn't sure what would happen if they reached me. Then my survival instincts took over and immediately shut off the channel. The elevator doors closed instantly and I was left unharmed but scared.

I didn't try channeling again until I had figured out what went wrong. I reread my book and there it was, a brief sentence warning me against doing exactly what I had done. For some reason, I had not remembered it. Since that time, I am very careful, repeat *very careful,* to only channel at a high, clear frequency in a place where I know I am safe.

Tonight in the hotel room, however, I am bored, and even though part of me doubts that I will be able to channel JO because I am not in a safe place, I decide to ask. Sitting on the bed, I cross my legs, straighten my back, close my eyes, and enter a state of meditation. When I am ready, I quickly send my thoughts to JO and ask if he wants to talk. By keeping the contact brief, I hope that if there are any malevolent spirits around, they will not have time to focus on us and harm our communication (like making a quick phone call in "the old days" and hanging up before anyone can trace it). His answer is immediate and succinct: "No. It is not safe." Then he shuts off the link and is gone. I got my answer. I will have to wait until I return home before contacting him again.

Dark Star

Excerpt from lyrics by Robert Hunter

DARK STAR CRASHES
POURING ITS LIGHT
INTO ASHES

REASON TATTERS
THE FORCES TEAR LOOSE
FROM THE AXIS

SEARCHLIGHT CASTING
FOR FAULTS IN THE
CLOUDS OF DELUSION

SHALL WE GO,
YOU AND I
WHILE WE CAN?
THROUGH
THE TRANSITIVE NIGHTFALL
OF DIAMONDS

MIRROR SHATTERS
IN FORMLESS REFLECTIONS
OF MATTER

GLASS HAND DISSOLVING
TO ICE-PETAL FLOWERS
REVOLVING

LADY IN VELVET
RECEDES
IN THE NIGHTS OF GOOD-BYE

SHALL WE GO,
YOU AND I
WHILE WE CAN?
THROUGH
THE TRANSITIVE NIGHTFALL
OF DIAMONDS

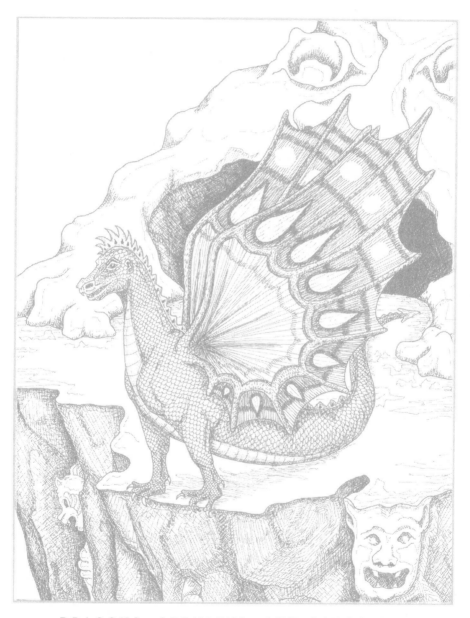

DRAGONS, GREMLINS, AND GARGOYLES

CHAPTER 14

Forces in the Universe

THURSDAY, SEPTEMBER 7, 1995

I RETURNED FROM MY TRIP LATE LAST NIGHT. NOW that I am back in the safety of my home, I am able to start communicating with JO again. It is early in the morning, a little too early considering the three-hour time-zone change I just had from the other direction. My mind tells me I should be up and doing business because it's ten A.M. in New York, but my body wants to stay snuggled up in bed because it's only seven A.M. here. However, I know JO wants to get going, so I drink a cup of hot tea, sit in my chair, and enter a state of meditation. When I am ready, JO initiates the conversation.

JO: Welcome back.

WW: Thanks.

JO: Your trip was good?

WW: Yes, and somewhat relaxing.

JO: Good. We will start this morning with new information: the forces at work in the Universe. Some call them good and evil. Some call them positive and negative. It all depends on the perspective of the beholder. Evil connotes fear. Negative does not. Many say evil does not exist, it is only negative that exists. I disagree. Evil is an aspect of the negative, but it does exist. Fear exists, and where there is fear there is a negative force creating and holding on to it. Evil and negative exist both within ourselves and without, as do good and positive. To deny the first would only be to give it power, to allow it to build in the dark until it quietly overcomes the light.

I agree. Evil exists, both within the Universe and within each of us. Although we don't often experience it firsthand in our "civilized" society, we see its presence daily on the television screen and in the media: wars, political manipulation, human and planetary degradation, murder, other crimes, and more. I have never had a truly evil experience on the physical level, only on the spiritual one, but this did not diminish its impact. Each time its psychic presence struck terror in my gut, and each time I was caught completely by surprise.

The scariest time was the night after Bob's dog, Otis, died in January 1987. Whenever Otis howled at the full moon, he appeared to be part wolf, but any relationship with wolves, as far as I could see, stopped there. I was wrong. As pets often do, Otis protected Bob both in the physical and in the psychic sense. As long as Otis was healthy, he was able to watch over Bob safely, but when Otis's health started to fail at the age of eighteen, his ability to protect Bob started to fail, too. A gradual decline began, slow at first but building in momentum like a boulder breaking loose from a cliff and crashing down the mountain, gaining speed. And like the boulder, Otis's decline ripped Bob from his foundation and dragged him down. The two were so closely connected that the only way out for Bob was Otis's death. On the afternoon that Otis died, Bob was devastated. He had reached the bottom and was overcome by emotions. He was also very vulnerable and totally unprotected, or so I thought.

That night, Bob managed to play the Dead's Chinese New Year concert at the Oakland Auditorium, as I mentioned earlier. It was an agonizing evening for him, but few in the audience knew that something traumatic had just happened. The only clue was when the band played "He's Gone." Traditionally, they perform this song to honor the death of a loved one, and Otis was so honored.

At the end of the show, I was still extremely concerned about Bob, so I told him that I would follow him home to make sure that everything was all right. The night was pitch dark, and when we arrived at his house, the energy surrounding it was equally dark, but I attributed that to Otis's death only hours before. Bob said that he would be fine, which I did not doubt, but I disliked the energy around him, so as I was leaving I said that I would be back before he left for the show the next day.

Darkness came early in January and the garden lights had not yet come on as I climbed the steps to his house. Looking up, I could see only one light on downstairs. Everything was strangely quiet. When I neared the top of the steps, a sense of evil foreboding swept over me and I was filled with terror. One reality merged seamlessly with another and I suddenly saw two snarling, crazed spirit wolves round the back corner of his house and charge ferociously toward me. Everything became slow motion. I could see their scruffy black coats, lean rippling muscles, and gleaming white fangs. Fire danced wildly in their shadowy eyes and saliva flecked from their snapping jaws as they gathered themselves to leap for my throat. My physical instinct was to turn and run—I knew they wanted to kill me—but I also knew that wouldn't help. They were spirits and I had to take a stand.

Moving aside my fear and panic, I placed both feet firmly on the ground and stretched my right arm straight out in front with its flat palm facing toward them. In my mind, I commanded: "Stop!" Their running stride broke as I continued, "I am Bob's sister. I come in love. He has invited me here." The two wolves slid to a stop and lowered their heads so they were staring me directly in the eyes. I stood still. The stench of evil rose from their backs like steam and I wondered why such terrifying beasts were suddenly prowling around my brother's house. The alpha wolf heard my thoughts and snarled back, "Otis is dead. He called us here to protect Bob." Again I said, "I am his sister. I come in love. Let me pass." They did not move but the tension in their bodies eased. Slowly, I climbed the last three steps to the porch and stood in front of them. Hounds from hell. I passed between their panting muzzles and fierce gaze, walked over to the sliding glass door which entered into the living room, and placed my hand on the handle. They did not move. Breathing deeply, I pulled the door open, entered the house, turned around, and slid the door shut. Outside, the spirit wolves took one last look at me before trotting down the steps to resume their protective rounds. Once I realized that I was safe, my whole body started to shake.

> *When negative or evil is felt or seen, it is best to look at it, understand it, and release its hold over you. It really is not that difficult if only you are able to hold the strong intent to do so, and if only you are willing to go through the process of release and learn from it.*

With pounding heart and trembling step, I walked over to the stairs and called up to Bob in his bedroom. He said that he needed to finish getting ready for the concert and would be right down. I went back to the living room and sat on a couch facing the sliding glass door so I could see if the spirit wolves returned. I had to understand what had just happened. As I waited for Bob, I breathed deeply to calm my fears and cleanse the feeling of evil that permeated my bones. I recalled that one of the wolves had said that Otis had called them to protect Bob. But why such evil? I tried to check with Otis's spirit, but I couldn't make contact, so I waited for Bob and watched the wolves pass by in the darkness.

When Bob finally came downstairs, I told him what had happened outside. I thought he would be surprised, but instead he calmly said, "Oh, you saw them."

"Yes, I saw them. They were going to kill me! What are they doing here?" My voice was rising.

"The wolves are my guardians."

"Why are they so evil?" I asked as a shiver of memory coursed through my body.

"They are not evil," Bob continued. "It only feels that way to you. When Otis was dying, a lot of negative feelings and fears broke loose. The weaker he became, the stronger the negative energy being released by him became. Over the years, he took on a lot of my negative energy from drugs and alcohol in order to keep me safe. But he couldn't keep me safe any longer. As he died, he had to release it. But he didn't want to leave me unprotected, so he called in the spirit wolves. They didn't harm you."

"No, they didn't. They just scared me to death! What the hell is going on here?"

"It'll be all right. We have to leave now. Don't worry," he added. Nothing more was said.

The two spirit wolves remained for several months. As Bob healed emotionally, so did the energy around the house. With time the sense of evil and negativity that I had experienced the first night faded. I gradually became comfortable with their presence and they with mine, and I grew to appreciate their power and protective strength. Before they left, I asked for two spirit wolves of my own to help protect me in times of danger. Now whenever I feel fear, I, too, call on the spirit wolves.

Many people look at dragons, gremlins, and gargoyles as embodying evil. In reality they do not. Like humans, there are those that have not been able yet to bring their darker aspects to the light. Their true purpose is not to scare mankind but to assist it. Deep within each of us there is a dungeon, a cave, where we hide our dragons, gremlins, and gargoyles. Because we do not acknowledge their presence within us, we make them physical by carving them in stone, writing about them, painting them. In many ways we bring their presence within us into physicality so that we may see them and, hopefully, acknowledge their place within us.

Nowadays, we even make movies about them. One of my favorite is *Dragonheart*. In it, the old dragon, Draco, hides deep in his cave because the people fear he is evil and want to kill him. In reality he is a very wise being who offers part of his heart and eventually his whole life to save the people and heal the land. In death, he is free at last to return to his kindred in the stars.

Like Draco, our own dragons lie hidden in dark caves deep inside, and we are the ones who have put them there. Like Draco, they yearn to return to the light and be free. Part of the healing process is releasing these emotional dragons. They represent aspects of our lives that we can't or don't want to look at, so we hide them away from sight. In my case, my dragon represented all those times in my life (lives) when I had given away my power to others, when I had played "the victim." Initially, I did it—I believed—in order to survive and be loved. I was "the good little girl," the young helping wife, the single woman focused on healing others, the chameleon who blended with other people's energy because her own was so undefined. But I reached a point in midlife when I realized that I didn't need these behaviors any longer. What I needed was to be me.

As I started taking my power back and becoming more centered, painful memories of disempowerment would rise up in me to be released. Being visual, I saw this process in my mind's eye. The dragon would awake within, groggy and angry after eons of abandonment, rise shakily to its feet, and climb out of its lightless lair. It would stop briefly at the opening of the cave to adjust its ancient eyes to the bombardment of brilliant light. Then slowly and stiffly it would move its shimmering iridescent body to the edge of the cliff, stretch out its gossamer wings to catch the gentle breeze, raise its long, lustrous neck toward the sun, and roar with anguish from the depths of its being. With each roar, long-hidden feelings of pain and sadness would be released. At times, I could even see flames shoot out from between its sharp, yellowed teeth, scorching the fresh, fragrant air.

Gradually the dragon and I became friends, then I became the dragon. As emotional blocks rose up from my inner cave, I was now the one who roared out in pain. Sometimes it would be in silence, sometimes it would be out loud, but roar I did. Then one day, goaded by the emotional hurt of a relationship, I became very angry and tired of feeling "the victim." Without thinking, I lashed out and grabbed for all my power with a vengeance. As I did this, I saw my dragon climb up from deep inside and stop at the cave's entrance to adjust its eyes. As its vision cleared, it looked around with a sinuous swing of its neck. In front of it spread verdant, tree-covered hills pocketed with patches of grassy fields. The bright sunlight created a landscape accented by shadows, and the electric blue sky lay back-to-back with the earth.

The dragon took its time, absorbing both the beauty of this sight with its sparkling eyes and the warmth of the sun on its shimmering scales. Then it moved slowly to the edge of the cliff. Flapping its expansive wings with strong, hard strokes, it let out a deafening roar that lasted for endless minutes. Flames of anger and hurt shot out, burning up in the light of day. Then when all of the painful memories had been released, the dragon became very still and peaceful. Looking around with a loving gaze, it stretched its wings to the sky and, much to my surprise, rose gracefully up and flew proudly away.

As it disappeared into the distance, I realized that I, too, was free. I had released my dragon and reclaimed my power.

The need at this time is to look within. Go deep. Go into the cave. Greet the dragon with love. Talk to it. Welcome it. Embrace it. Release it into the light. For too many eons they have chosen to remain hidden within because mankind chose to forget their good, positive aspects. Mankind made them models for their fear. Now, if you look at these images of dragons, gremlins, and gargoyles throughout your history, look at them not as subjects to be feared but as mirrors of your inner self. They are there, on the churches, in the myths, to remind you to go within. They are aspects of you that need to be integrated in order for you to become complete.

This may confuse some of you. Others may not believe it. But once again, the keys to "en-light-en-ment" are within you. All you need to do is see them and allow them to help you unlock the doors.

The Earth is like a large house with many doors, and the keys to these doors are scattered all around. Your intent will find these keys, will recognize them by their "feel," and your courage will enable you to use them. Shift your gaze. Shift your consciousness. Look anew at life and all that surrounds you. The keys are there. Reach out and grab them.

This is enough for now, little one. I am glad we have been able to resume our work. It is important, and there is not much time (time is also a key). We will talk again tomorrow.

WW: Go with love, Jer.

Black Muddy River

Excerpt from lyrics by Robert Hunter

WHEN IT SEEMS LIKE THE NIGHT WILL LAST FOREVER
AND THERE'S NOTHING LEFT TO DO BUT COUNT THE YEARS
WHEN THE STRINGS OF MY HEART START TO SEVER
AND STONES FALL FROM MY EYES INSTEAD OF TEARS

I WILL WALK ALONE BY THE BLACK MUDDY RIVER
AND DREAM ME A DREAM OF MY OWN
I WILL WALK ALONE BY THE BLACK MUDDY RIVER
AND SING ME A SONG OF MY OWN
AND SING ME A SONG OF MY OWN

THE RIVER OF LIFE

Childhood

fRIDAY, septeMBeR 8, 1995

JO IS THERE ON THE FRINGE OF MY AWARENESS AS I
meditate, but he is not pushing today. He is actually waiting patiently.
A sense of calm and peace surrounds him.

JO: Are you ready now, little one?

WW: Yes, I am ready.

*JO: The thought just came to you as you were coming out of
meditation: childhood. You were picking up on my energies.
That is what we will discuss today.*

*Childhood can be a time of joy, laughter, innocence, and
fun. It can also be a time of great pain and hardship. Each
individual experiences his or her childhood differently, based
upon the lessons that they have come to Earth to learn.*

*In Jerry's case, his father died when he was very young.
He saw it happen. This was an incredible shock to his*

emotional, psychological system although he was not con-
sciously aware of it at the time. As you know with your own
parents' death when you were younger, you do not have the
tools developed yet to deal with and process these deep
shocks.

A deep shock is not necessarily the result of a tragic
occurrence. It might also result from something that might
seem quite normal to others, such as a mother leaving her
young child to go back to work. This would bring up issues
of abandonment for the child if that is what it has come to
Earth to resolve.

Whether we are aware of it or not, the fear of abandonment lies
at the root, the core, of many of our unhealthy behaviors. Some of my
own fears of abandonment go back to birth. I didn't discover this
until I was talking to a friend who had just gone back to her own birth
through hypnotic regression. She told me how much she had learned
about herself and I told her it sounded like a great experience, but I
didn't have any interest in doing it myself. When she asked me what
memories I had of my own birth, a sense of anger rose up and I said:
"None!" She looked at me intently but said nothing; however, her
look did register that there was more to my reply than I wanted to
admit.

I couldn't forget my reaction to her question, so I finally decided
to explore the issue using visualization. I entered a state of meditation, and when I was ready, I asked to be taken back to my birth so I
could understand my feeling of anger. I was born at Children's
Hospital in San Francisco by cesarean section, so I started by visual-
izing a hospital room with my mother lying on the operating table. At
this point, my visualization took on a life of its own. The next thing I
saw was the doctor pulling me out of my mother's womb. There was
no passage through the birth canal, no time to transition from the
dark warmth and security of her familiar body to my arrival in this

brightly lit, sterile, strange room filled with the smell of medicine. As I dangled from the doctor's outstretched hands, I instinctively looked around for my mother and father, whom I had expected to greet me with love and joy. Instead all I saw was this huge form covered in green material with only the eyes uncovered to show me that it was human. Why weren't they here? Where were they? What went wrong? These thoughts coursed through my mind. Then without warning, the doctor turned me upside down and slapped me on my bottom. It both hurt and shocked me, and I began to cry in pain and fear. Then the thought occurred to me that I hadn't done anything wrong—how dare he abuse me like that!—and I became angry, very angry, and cried even more.

As a newborn child, I didn't understand that my mother was lying unconscious from the anesthestics used in the cesarean operation, that my father was anxiously pacing in the nearby waiting room because the hospital in those days would not allow him to be present at my birth, and that the well-intentioned doctor only slapped me to make sure that I was breathing and healthy. All I perceived was the pain: I was alone, cold, abandoned, and betrayed. And my reaction was one of deep anger.

The trauma of this experience stayed in my subconscious memory and seriously influenced my adult behavior. I looked for safety and security in a partner so that I would not feel alone; I often had a "net" (a potential partner on the back burner) so that I would not feel abandoned if my current relationship ended; and I felt that if anything ever went wrong I could fix it myself, I didn't need to depend on anyone else because they might fail or betray me. The regression back to my birth helped to reveal the reason for many of my behaviors. Now I could look at them more clearly and start the healing process.

Once again, in Jerry's case, seeing the death of his father not only brought up issues of abandonment, it also brought up his physical fear of dying, on the one hand, and the reminder that he didn't like all the pain that one can experience here on Earth, on the other. His fears, his issues, kept him from being fully present in his body, from fully expressing himself while here. But instead of dealing with these issues as he grew older, he chose to hang on to them. He had decided that it was easier for him to deal with this Earth experience by being detached from it. He lived with one foot in this world and one in the next, ready at any time to exit into spirit. The drugs, the lack of respect for his physical body, were tools that he used to keep himself in this state.

I can relate to this. I didn't want to be fully present in my body either, because then I would have to feel my emotions, and if I felt my emotions, sooner or later I would feel my pain. So whenever I found myself in an emotionally uncomfortable situation, I would either keep my attention on the person but detach my mind and let it wander, or I would turn my face up to the right, look into space with my eyes, and answer the question from a purely mental, objective point of view. I never used drugs, though. I didn't like losing control.

Jerry went through recurrent stages in life when he would clean up, go off drugs, eat right, work out, and get healthy. But he could never stay healthy. For one reason or another, he would start doing drugs again. The day before he died, he had checked himself into a drug rehabilitation center because this time he was determined to get clean and stay clean. This was going to be the last time that he was going through this struggle, and he was right. It was.

This is not what Jerry came down here to do. He had decided, when he was still in spirit, that he would try to resolve and release his fear of abandonment and his fear of death in the physical. He chose, as we all do, the primary experiences in life that will set these lessons in motion.

However, he was not able, throughout his life, to resolve these issues. He refused to let go of his tie to the spirit, to trust fully in his Earth experience, to surrender to the higher wisdom of his lessons, to become one with the flow of the Universe. He maintained his duality, he remained divided, he remained apart. Any attempt he made on a conscious level to heal himself he sabotaged, because on a deeper level, where our source of power resides, he was afraid to go through the pain that it would take to change.

Jerry will now have another opportunity, or should I say other opportunities, to resolve and release these fears. We all have as many opportunities as we need, for time is not linear. One life does not follow another. We exist. We learn. We grow toward oneness with the light that is God/All That Is. We cannot be destroyed. And there are many ways to learn our lessons. We are unlimited beings who can decide, often with impartial guidance from those close to us both in the spiritual and physical realms, how we wish to grow, to learn, to become "enlightened." We decide, on a deep, primal level, what is best for us.

Just because Jerry left the Earth plane without having accomplished some of his objectives does not mean that he was a failure. Mankind has a warped sense of what is success and what is failure. There is no failure. *All is success, because we learn from everything we do. We might not like what we learn, but we learn just the same. It is the learning, the knowledge, for which we strive. How we go about getting it, and how we process it, is up to us. So often what we think as humans is a failure, a disaster, is, from the perspective of the oversoul, an incredible success because of the vast amounts of learning received from that experience.*

Once again, shift your focus. Look within. What have you learned or what opportunities do you have to learn from each experience in life? Death. Abandonment. These are not crises. These are not disasters. These are keys to growth. See what they truly are and use them wisely: to grow, to expand, to become one with your true self, who is patiently waiting there under the layers of your fears to be free to embrace you in the physical as it does in the spirit.

Our communication is over for the day, little one. It has been good. I am beginning to feel more at peace as I discuss these issues with you. There is more, but we are starting to draw to a close. The rest is coming together well. You will know what I am talking about when it is time (there is that word time, *again). Go in peace, dear one. Go in love.*

WW: Go in peace, Jer. Go in love. I'll talk to you tomorrow.

JO's mood, his energy, has shifted. I realize now that during our talks he has been releasing much of his own pain and frustration. He sees so much from his perspective. He wants so badly to help, to make a difference in people's lives, to transform the burden of negativity that surrounds the Earth and impacts the Universe. He has been waiting a long time for this opportunity. No wonder he has been impatient.

Then the thought occurs to me. JO was connected to Jerry in the physical as he is now in the spirit. Maybe these feelings of pain and frustration originated from Jerry on Earth and are now being processed and released by his oversoul. As with JO and myself, the link, the energy, flows both ways.

Box of Rain

Excerpt from lyrics by Robert Hunter

walk out of any doorway
feel your way, feel your way
like the day before
maybe you'll find direction
around some corner
where it's been waiting to meet you—
what do you want me to do,
to watch for you while you're sleeping?
well, please don't be surprised
when you find me dreaming, too

Look into any eyes
you find by you, you can see
clear through to another day
i know it's been seen before
through other eyes on other days
while going home—
what do you want me to do,
to do for you to see you through?
it's all a dream we dreamed
one afternoon long ago

walk into splintered sunlight
inch your way through dead dreams
to another land
maybe you're tired and broken
your tongue is twisted
with words half spoken
and thoughts unclear—
what do you want me to do,
to do for you to see you through?
a box of rain will ease the pain
and love will see you through

it's just a box of rain
i don't know who put it there
believe it if you need it
or leave it if you dare
but it's just a box of rain
or a ribbon for your hair
such a long, long time to be gone
and a short time to be there

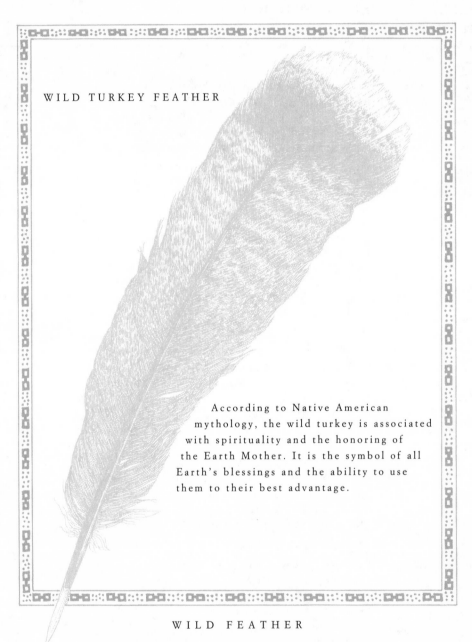

WILD TURKEY FEATHER

According to Native American
mythology, the wild turkey is associated
with spirituality and the honoring of
the Earth Mother. It is the symbol of all
Earth's blessings and the ability to use
them to their best advantage.

WILD FEATHER

Today

saturday, september 9, 1995

Softly, from the outer limit of my awareness, I feel JO reaching into my meditation.

JO: It is time.

WW: I'm almost ready.

One minute later.

JO: It is time, dear one.

This is said with a sense of peace and love. The feelings of pressure, frustration, and impatience are gone.

WW: Yes, I am ready.

JO: Today…do you notice I start our sessions with "today"?
[He smiles.]

I smile because today is every day. It is all time. It is the now in which all exists. It is the moment of ecstasy. It is the beginning of all eternity. It is the ever-expanding infinite.

This moment of which we speak is the moment in which our power exists. Without taking action in the moment, there is no action. The point of power is NOW. It is not tomorrow. It is not yesterday. It is today. Now. This moment.

That is why I start with the word today. *It is to establish the present firmly in your mind so that you become fully focused on what is going on* now.

This is how each and every one of you should lead your lives. Today. In the moment. Now. Only by doing this are you able to free yourself enough to feel the ebb and flow of the energies around you. When you are in tune with these energies, they carry you like a feather on the breeze, without strings to bind or control you, to float to the rhythm of the universal song.

When you are in touch, fully, with the ongoing present, your life flows. Struggle is no longer struggle, for you have let go of your fears that led you to try to control your life. Now you have surrendered to a deep trust and faith in All That Is.

Yes, there is a higher plan in which we all participate, consciously or unconsciously. This does not negate our free will, our spontaneity, our creativity. It actually enhances these aspects of self, because you no longer waste your precious energy on trying to control that which cannot be controlled. By becoming an active, supportive part of the whole, your individuality becomes accentuated, not annihilated, and life becomes more supportive of you and your needs (may I remind you, not your wants or desires, but your needs).

There is a flow of energy in all that you do, as there is a melody that weaves through a song. Reach out with your heart and with your soul, shift your gaze, and touch this flow. It is refreshing, it is cool, it is clear, it is infinite, coming from the unseen and going to the unseen. You, as humans, cannot know and see all. You are limited by the lower frequencies of the Earth plane. However, you can have a feeling of knowing, *which comes from deep inside and guides your actions without the interference of the mind. You know. In this moment, you are. In this moment, you act.*

This state of knowingness cannot exist without deep trust and faith, both in yourself and in the forces of the Universe. Surrender your fears. Surrender your need to struggle. Surrender your beliefs that limit you and are no longer needed. Surrender to your true self that waits for you within.

You are not your mother's child, your child's mother, your father's favorite, your spouse's loved one, your boss's employee. You are not identified by where you live, the car you drive, the amount of money in your bank account. Your true value is not determined by what your job or salary is. These are all external objects that act as mirrors to show you what you need to learn. Your beliefs, your need to learn certain things, set these mirrors up throughout your life so that you can look at them and learn from the experiences they bring into your life. However, be very clear, they are not you. *Who you truly are lies deep within, not without. Discover who you are, honor it, embrace it. All that is outside of you will shift and change as you shift into a deeper consciousness. That which you unveil has always been there, you just have not looked for it and therefore have not found it.*

The threads of the Universe unite us all. The clearer we become as individuals, the higher our frequency, the more that we are able to embrace our true selves, the more light, joy, love, and humor—yes, humor—we will be able to hold within us and radiate out to others.

But this can only be done with each today, with each moment, with each now that we live. Do not wait. Wait for what? All is now. Reach out. Grab on to the flow of energies that surround you. Go freely where it takes you. Go in love. Go in peace.

We will talk again tomorrow, dear one. My deepest love is with you and all mankind who have the courage to take this journey. Herein lies your freedom.

WW: Thanks, Jer. I see your thoughts as you speak, and they are beautiful.

Attics of My Life

Lyrics by Robert Hunter

IN THE attics of my Life
fuLL of cLoudy DReams unReaL
fuLL of tastes no tongue can know
and Lights no eye can see
    when there was no eaR to heaR
    you sang to me

I have spent my Life
seeking aLL that's stILL unsung
bent my eaR to heaR the tune
and cLosed my eyes to see
    when theRe weRe no stRings to pLay
    you pLayed to me

IN THE book of Love's own DReam
wheRe aLL the pRint is bLood
wheRe aLL the pages aRe my Days
and aLL my Lights gRow oLd
    when I had no wings to fLy
    you fLew to me

you
fLew
to me

IN THE secRet space of DReams
wheRe I DReaming Lay amazeD
when the secRets aLL aRe toLD
and the petaLs aLL unfoLD
    when theRe was no DReam of mine
    you DReameD of me

BARU, THE CROCODILE

CHAPTER 17

Adventure

MONDAY, SEPTEMBER 11, 1995

IN WORKING CLOSELY WITH JO OVER THE PAST MONTH, I find we have reached a state of comfortable familiarity, like an old married couple who have known each other through the ups and downs of a lifetime. It has become a dance where our energies ebb and flow together, gently embracing and guiding each other. Sometimes I lead, sometimes he leads, but we are both moving in rhythm.

JO: [Smiling] *I am waiting, little one.*

WW: *Good, Jer.*

One minute later I am ready, and...

JO: *We shall begin. Today we will discuss adventure.*

WW: *Adventure?*

JO: Yes, adventure. The sense of adventure resides within the soul of every man and every woman. Otherwise you would not have chosen the exciting journey to Earth. To come down here, to open yourself up to new experiences, new feelings, new sensations in the physical, requires an innate sense of adventure. Even those who consider themselves shy and timid have an incredible amount of strength and courage within them, only they are not consciously aware of it yet. You still allow the illusion of who you think you are to control the reality of who you truly are.

An adventure can be a trip around the world or a trip to the grocery store. It can be as tangible as an airplane or as intangible as a dream. You can go out and seek it, or it can come in and seek you. It can be a journey to outer space, or it can be a journey to your inner space. On this adventure, there are no mistakes, only lessons. Whatever we experience enables us to grow in knowledge and wisdom, even if it is simply the statement "I will never do that again." At the very least you have had the experience and have learned that it is something you don't wish to repeat. If the experience cycles back to you in a different form, then look at it closely because there is something more for you to learn.

All in the physical is illusion. You have created it as the "playing field" for your adventure. All on Earth have agreed to certain ground rules of the game in order to come down here, but it is actually our creation to help us learn the lessons that we have come here to learn.

Playing field. What a great image. JO looks at Earth as a playing field for the game of life. This image is a lot better than the one I had of Earth being a classroom and we the students, which suggests that we have to study hard, do what the teacher says, and pass all of the tests in order to graduate to the next higher grade. It also sets up the possibility of failure. There is no failure. There is only learning, and from learning comes growth. Play, not struggle—I like it.

Certain ground rules. Yes, in order to play the game, we, as sentient beings, have to agree to abide by certain ground rules before we incarnate on Earth. For each of us, the game is to successfully accomplish our life's purpose or mission while here, and in order for us to have a common playing field on which to do this, we have to abide by some basic rules.

For instance, one rule is to forget. In order to play the game seriously, we have to believe that the illusion of what we have created is, from our Earthly perspective, our reality. Reality now becomes defined by what we physically perceive with one or more of our five senses: taste, smell, hearing, touch, and sight. One of the challenges of the game is to remember what we have chosen to forget.

Another rule is to obey the law of gravity. This creates the "ground" for the playing field. Gravity keeps our physical bodies in a constant, stable relationship to the Earth and everything around us. From this foundation we can experience action and reaction.

A third rule is that we accept the concept of time. Nowadays we have calendars and watches and even computers to let us know what day and time it is. Time gives us a sense of past, present, and future by which we can determine what moves we need to make in the game, when we should make them, and how successful they are.

A fourth rule is that we have free will. This is a core truth. The problem is that many people don't believe this and think that it is an illusion. They blame their problems on fate or karma or anything and everything outside of themselves. If only they would take responsibility for their actions, they would have a lot more fun and creativity in how they make their plays. As long as we abide by the ground rules within the guidelines of our mission, we can play the game any way we want.

How can something be real, in the true meaning of the word, if it does not last? All that is physical here on Earth eventually changes and dissolves or transforms. Only the spirit remains for eternity. The spirit always has been and always will be, no matter what form it takes, what environment it lives in, what planet or realm it inhabits. The spirit is what is real. *The rest is illusion. But all is energy.*

Energy, as mentioned previously, is the basis of all the Universes, of all creation. Energy takes on and takes off an incredible number of forms and expressions in order to learn and to grow. This knowledge and growth, once acquired, is never lost. It may be forgotten, it may be overshadowed, but it is never lost.

People have acknowledged the existence of universal energy for thousands of years. For more than five thousand years, the spiritualists of India have believed in *prana*. Prana is the basic component and source of all life, existing and moving through all forms. The Chinese, as early as the third millennium B.C., called this force *ch'i*, the vital energy that composed and permeated all matter, both animate and inanimate. The belief in universal energy, however, is not just limited to the Eastern religions. Over the past one hundred years, it has also become accepted in our Western scientific community.

To give a few examples, in the 1800s the mathematician Helmont postulated that there is a universal fluid or vital spirit that penetrates all bodies and is not of corporeal matter. In 1905, Albert Einstein published his theory of relativity. This theory stated that time is relative, being neither linear nor absolute, that space is not three-dimensional, and that space and time are connected to form a four-dimensional "space-time" continuum. As a consequence, scientists began to realize that energy and matter of any type are interchangeable. Mass is just a different form of energy. From the 1930s through the 1950s, Dr. Wilhelm Reich, a psychiatrist and colleague of

Freud's, studied universal energy, which he called "orgone," by using the latest electronic and medical technology. With it, he was able to observe this energy pulsating in the sky and around all animate and inanimate forms. In 1964, the physicist J. S. Bell published mathematical proof, called Bell's theorem, that went one step further than Einstein's theory of relativity. Bell stated that subatomic particles are connected in some way beyond space and time so that anything that happens to one particle affects all other particles. Everything in the Universe is connected by a form of energy. Today scientists continue with their exploration of and experiments with universal energy, and many scientists are now incorporating Eastern spiritual beliefs into their own Western scientific observations.

> *Since this knowledge* [about the nature of energy] *still exists, it is our opportunity to take the time, go within, and* remember *that knowledge. Not everyone is the same, but working to the fullest of our abilities with the fullest extent of our knowledge will benefit the whole. In our immediate case, this whole is mankind and planet Earth. In a more expanded sense, it is our Universe and all the Universes that exist, which are a part of All That Is.*
>
> *To return to adventure, when you are on an adventure, your senses are more heightened. Your adventure may create in you many new feelings, which, because you are in an unfamiliar environment, you experience more intensely. Stimuli bombard you. You look at things differently. Your belief structures shift and change. When you are on an adventure, anything can happen. There is no sense of safety or security because the adventure implies new discoveries, which become integrated within the self.*

The first adventure that I vividly remember was when I was three years old. It was a brilliant, rich spark of color on an otherwise gray palette. This, as far as I was concerned, was when my life really began. As I recall it now, the screen inside my head is blank, then suddenly the light comes on and I see my mother and me riding a quiet brown horse along a trail that wanders through the lush green meadow in Squaw Valley, California, near Lake Tahoe. It is summertime. The bright sunlight warms my little body and the smell of the horse's sweat rises up into my nostrils. My mother had ridden since she was a young girl, so she was very comfortable on the horse. We sat together in the Western saddle, I snuggled between the horn and her body. Her strong, sleeveless right arm was wrapped around my waist to keep me safe, while the left hand held the leather reins and guided the horse. The rhythm of the horse's hooves as they hit the hard dirt path lulled me into a state of bliss. I was happy.

Suddenly there was a movement in the grass alongside the path— it might have been a snake—and the horse spooked. In an instant, he bolted forward, my mother jerked the reins back hard to stop him, and the right rein snapped, its loose end flying up and hitting him in the face. In the next instant, he was galloping wildly down the trail, jumping small streams, heading for what he probably thought was safety in the dense pine forest ahead. I am sure it didn't help that I was screaming from the thrill and excitement of the run. Fortunately, my mother did not lose her grip on me, on the saddle, on the single rein, or on the situation. From experience, she knew to pull hard on the remaining rein to turn the horse's head to the left. Where the head goes, the body follows. As the horse started to circle, he had to slow his pace and gradually she was able to bring him safely under control. At this point, the light goes off and my inner screen goes gray again. It was one of the most exhilarating experiences of my life, and since that time I have been passionately involved with horses.

Adventure is a part of us that is critical to our growth. It opens us up. It changes us. We become more "alive" for the experience. Along with joy, love, and peace, adventure is an integral part of our being. As I have said, you would not be down here if you did not have a sense of adventure.

One of the most life-altering adventures that I ever had was my trip to Australia with Bob in October 1992 to do research for our children's book *Baru Bay*. We had made arrangements through Kerrie Jarvis, a close Australian friend of ours who was with us on the trip, to visit an Aboriginal community along the north coast of Australia. Just as our Indian reservations in the United States are governed by Indians, these communities are governed by the Aboriginals. No one is allowed in without an invitation. I had been trying for six months to get this permission through the Aboriginal affairs department of the federal government to no avail. Luckily, Kerrie and the universal world of music came to our rescue.

Kerrie and her husband, Wane, were concert promoters who had worked with the internationally famous Aboriginal rock band Yothu Yindi, which in the Gumatj dialect means "child and mother." The leader of the group is a wonderful and talented man, Mandawuy Yunupingu, who in 1992 was named Australian of the Year for his efforts to heal the racial rift between the white and the black people, as exemplified by the band's members (both indigenous and white) and the lyrics and beat of their music (combining traditional instrumentation and songs with contemporary Western instruments and arrangements).

Kerrie talked to Mandawuy and arranged for us to meet in San Francisco in July when his band played at Slim's. Bob was on tour with the Dead, so I talked with Mandawuy and explained what we wanted to do, and asked for permission to visit his community. He knew nothing about me, but fortunately he had been listening to the Grateful Dead in the farthest reaches of Arnhem Land since the late 1970s. Based upon Bob's musical reputation, a tentative invitation was extended. I say tentative because we did not know for sure until three hours before we boarded the plane in Cairns, Australia, to fly to Gove, the closest airport to Mandawuy, whether or not we would be allowed to enter.

We had arrived in Cairns the previous week and everything looked good for our visit, so we booked our flight. Then Mandawuy called and told us that one of the elders had died and that the community was closed to outsiders during the funeral ceremonies. He was not sure when it would reopen, but thought it might be in four or five days. Bob and I checked our schedule and fortunately we were able to move a few things around; then we waited. On the morning of the fifth day, Mandawuy called and told us to get on the next plane to Gove. We booked our flight and were on our way.

We stayed with the Gumatj people for four days. It doesn't seem like a long period of time, but for us it felt like an eternity. So much happened on so many different levels of which we were not conscious that by the time we flew back to Cairns we felt psychically "fried." We had not only crossed the physical border into Gumatj territory, we had also, without knowing it, crossed the invisible border into the Dreamtime.

People often ask me if the Dreamtime is real. Believe me, it is. To give a very simplistic explanation, the Dreamtime is a state of existence beyond our concept of time where the elders of creation live. These spirit beings are an intrinsic part of the Aboriginals' existence, interacting with them on a continual basis because they exist not only in a higher realm but also in the physical realm. To the Aboriginal people, a line of hills might represent the Rainbow Serpent (the sacred source of creation) and a group of boulders the serpent's eggs. Each clan also has a totem, an object or animal that is a symbol of the clan. These totems are also from the Dreamtime. For the Gumatj, their totem is *baru,* the crocodile, a very powerful creature who brought the gift of fire to their people.

Where we were, watches had no use or relevance. After the first day we tuned in to what I can only describe as the flow of the

Universe and stopped asking what time we were going to do this or that, what time we should meet, when we would get there. Everything happened when it was supposed to happen. The sense of being one with the flow was so strong that it was almost tangible. It shifted our perspective of reality. Time warped. Stress vanished. We moved in harmony with life.

Out of the rich mosaic of experiences that Bob and I had, the one that impressed me the most deeply was the "cleansing ceremony." My understanding of this ceremony was that the community honored the deceased elder one last time by symbolically, and literally, cleansing themselves of her death, thereby freeing her to move on with her journey to the Dreamtime and allowing them to return to their daily lives. Traditionally, this is the last ceremony for the deceased and is performed four days after the burial. This placed it right in the middle of our visit.

After discussing our presence with the other elders, Mandawuy and his brother Galarrwuy, the "king" of the clan (named Australian of the Year in the 1980s), asked us to attend. We arrived at their cluster of homes along the beach in the early afternoon and got out of our car. Bob and another friend, Bill Carter, hung out with the men, smoking each other's cigarettes and drinking beer and soft drinks. Kerrie and I stayed with them briefly, then we asked for permission to walk around. We wandered over to a group of women sitting on the side of a small hill near one of the homes. They were talking and laughing; one was making a necklace out of bright red and black seeds. We chatted with them for a while, then moved on. Further along we stopped to talk to one of the elders, the only one present that day, as he sat on a blanket in the shade of a large tree. He was very old and arthritic, but he enjoyed our conversation and told us several tribal stories in a clear yet halting voice. When he finished, Kerrie walked back to join Bob and Bill, and I strolled down the beach to join three young boys who were happily playing with the only commercial toy in the community—a plastic beach ball. The tide was out, leaving a vast stretch of moist, hard sand on which to run.

The afternoon lazed along until Mandawuy called us over. The ceremony was about to begin, so he asked Kerrie and me to go up and sit with the women on the hillside while Bob and Bill joined the men at the sacred hut. The hut was made of eucalyptus planks, with a corrugated tin roof and a wood door at one end. It was built on the upper slope of the beach in the shape of a diamond, each side approximately ten feet long and seven feet high. The diamond was their sacred symbol for *baru,* the crocodile, totem of their clan. From where I sat, I could see a green garden hose running down the hill from a house and into the hut. The door to the hut was closed, but it was easy to hear women and children talking and laughing inside. The men took their places sitting on the sandy ground along the uphill side of the hut while Kerrie and I sat with the rest of the women approximately thirty feet behind them.

Soon several of the men started to play their yidakis (commonly referred to as didgeridoos) and the rest joined in clapping with their bilma (hardwood clap-sticks) and hands. Then they began a tribal chant. Some of the men stood, jumping up and down on one leg, while others remained seated. As the men sang and danced to this primal beat, the women and children inside the hut splashed in the hose water, laughing and singing. At a certain point, Galarrwuy looked up at Kerrie and me and motioned with his hand for us to come down. We didn't understand at first because we knew that no women were allowed, but he continued to wave and so we left the blanket and walked down the slope, where we stopped behind the men. Then he motioned us to sit and be silent. We could observe more closely but not actively participate.

When the tribal chant was over, the door to the sacred hut opened and all the women and children came streaming out single file and walked up the hill following the hose line. They were fully dressed but soaked to their skin with water and soapsuds. When they had all left the hut, the cleansing ceremony was over and the group of men disbanded.

Kerrie and I looked at each other. Why had we been invited to join the men? Seeing Galarrwuy still in his chair, we walked over, sat down on the sand in front of him, and asked. He looked at us kindly and said, "The elders told me to."

The only elder we had seen was still sitting under the tree. He had not moved since we had talked with him earlier that afternoon.

"What do you mean, Galarrwuy? What elders?" I queried.

"The ones up there," he said, pointing to the sky.

Kerrie and I were even more confused now. "Where?" Kerrie asked.

"Up there. In the Dreamtime," he answered patiently.

"In the Dreamtime?" we both asked incredulously.

"Yes, the elders of the Dreamtime tell me what to do and how to act. All that I do is follow their orders. They told me to ask you down to join the ceremony, so I did."

Having a hard time grasping what he was saying, I continued, "How do they talk to you?"

"In my head," he said, and with that he got up and walked away. End of conversation.

What had appeared as a simple ceremony to an outsider such as myself was indeed very sacred. On a conscious level I only understood what had happened based upon what I had seen, but on an unconscious level I was highly aware that the elders of the Dreamtime had taken a serious interest in our presence. Once again, I sensed them tearing at our old belief structures and altering our concept of reality. I had a feeling then that I would never be the same, but I didn't know how. It wasn't until we got home and I started working on *Baru Bay* that I realized I now had a deeper sense of connection with nature and the divine. I felt a part of the web of life, but instead of losing my individuality, I was enhanced by it. I could sense more clearly who I was both as an individual and as part of the whole. I

continued to walk with the elders in the Dreamtime and never fully
returned to the fast-paced, stressed-out life that I had been leading
before the trip.

*It is important, as you approach the beginning of each
day, to approach it as an adventure. What new things will
you learn today? What new paths will you discover? What
new experiences will you have? In what ways will you
remember your true self? What will be revealed to you?*

*As on any adventure, keep your senses alive, keep your
awareness heightened. Embrace each moment. Learn from
all that happens. Do not be complacent, for in complacency
comes destruction, a deadening of the senses, an annihila-
tion, no matter how gradual and "safe," of the life force.*

*Live! Feel! Explore! Learn! Move forward into each
day, each moment, each now, with a bright eye, an alert
body, a seeking mind, an open, loving spirit to embrace what
life has to offer you. Be alive! You have come down here for
adventure, now find it. This journey may start with outward
awareness, but all will help you to focus within. The greatest journey, the greatest adventure, is that which awaits each
and every one of you within yourselves. Go now, little one.
This day offers you great adventure. Embrace it!*

*WW: Thank you. Your words are so true. Today is definitely
going to be an adventure, and I am looking forward to it.
Take care, dear one.*

JO: We will talk again tomorrow. Go in love. Go in peace.

Terrapin Station

Excerpt from lyrics by Robert Hunter

INSPIRATION move me BRIGHTLY
LIGHT THE SONG WITH SENSE AND COLOR,
HOLD AWAY DESPAIR
MORE THAN THIS I WILL NOT ask
faced WITH mysteries DARK AND VAST
statements JUST seem VAIN at Last
some RISE, some faLL, some cLImB
to GET to TERRAPIN

COUNTING STARS BY CANDLELIGHT
aLL ARE DIM BUT ONE IS BRIGHT:
THE SPIRAL LIGHT Of VENUS
RISING fIRST AND SHINING BEST,
from THE NORTHWEST CORNER
Of a BRAND-NEW CRESCENT MOON
CRICKETS AND CICADAS SING
a RARE AND DIffERENT TUNE

YIN-YANG JERRY

Creation

tuesDay, septemBeR 12, 1995

THE PROCESS OF EARLY-MORNING MEDITATION HAS become a ritual for both of us. We are in sync today and the connection flows easily. JO is pleasant, warm, and humorous.

JO: All right, little one. Shall we begin?

WW: Okay, Jer.

JO: In the beginning, there was the beginning. I know this sounds very profound [slight laugh], but it is necessary to understand this concept in order to understand the creation of life and your position within this creation.

The big bang theory is pretty close to correct, but the scientists do not take into consideration the participation of God/All That Is in this action.

The big bang theory is a scientific explanation for the creation of the Universe. At first, all is chaos. Then from the midst of chaos comes a cosmic bang. An explosion of "something" lights up the dark, endless void and the Universe is formed instantaneously. Out of vast, drifting clouds of hydrogen gas and dust emerge primitive forms of life. Stars and planets take shape. Evolution begins. However, JO feels that this explanation is incomplete. It lacks God.

In the beginning [JO continues], *there was God, an all-powerful creative force whose purpose was to grow through the expression of love. I will explain this in simple terms. In order to learn and grow, God created other, or duality, because it is only in having other, or duality, that we can be stimulated, challenged, and thereby learn. As a means of creating other, God created energies that—because they were a part of God—also had the ability to create. Since all was of God, whatever these energies, and the energies that they created, and the energies that these new ones created on into infinity did, God would be able to learn from the experiences of these energies in their growth and expansion.*

In this process of creating duality, God encouraged these energies that were of Him to come together with incredible power and release this power into the Universes. Upon this release, your Universe, your galaxy, your solar system, and your planet Earth were formed. All of this, however, because it originated from the God source, was and is still a part of God. As mankind has God within him, so do the monkeys, horses, rocks, trees, water, atoms, and everything that exists on all dimensions.

Please note that on Earth, even though all matter has a spirit and is alive and evolves in its own fashion, only mankind has a soul. It is only mankind that exists in duality, separate in its perception from God. It is through the growth and evolution of the soul within each of us, over many incarnations, that we are able to move from this experience of duality and "re-member" our original state of oneness.

Creation is an amazing force that also exists within each of us. So is love. These positive, dynamic forces can be expressed when we get in touch with the God that is within us, that is us. Those who live in negativity have not recognized and embraced the God self within. It does not mean that because of the harm or pain that they might cause others that they do not have this God force. It only means that they have not yet found it and embraced it as a part of their true selves.

This is sad, from our higher perspective, because each soul, each creation, has limitless beauty when it is in touch with its true self. As we on this higher plane look down on Earth, we see and hear an incredible symphony of sound, light, and color. The only mar to this light show and concert are the dark notes and pictures presented and played by man when he is out of touch with his own vibration.

When mankind is out of touch with its own vibration, this discordant resonance is not only picked up by other people, but it is also picked up by our planet and impulsed out to all connected parts in the Universe, adversely affecting the harmony and "music of the spheres." This is very unfortunate for us, because based upon the principles of resonance, this discordant vibration bounces back to us and we experience its negative impact as earthquakes, floods, plagues, solar storms, and more, thereby enabling us to fully experience in the physical state what we consciously or unconsciously project in our emotional and mental states. It is important to keep in mind that our thoughts are alive, and by the process of thinking them we express them to the world. Positive thoughts create positive experiences. Negative thoughts create negative experiences. Mankind is a cocreator with God/All That Is.

> *On Earth, only man, with all his power, uses this power to break away from the laws of the Universe, to create negativity and destruction. All other beings abide by these laws because they recognize and honor their oneness with All That Is.*
>
> *The purpose of mankind's negativity is to create duality from which we can learn and grow. However, we do not want to get stuck in this state of negativity, which mankind is doing right now, because then those who are negative resist the change and learning that is presented to them on a regular basis as part of our normal growth process, and become blocked or stuck. This then blocks the flow and movement of the energies on Earth, which expand outward to affect the solar system, galaxy, Universe, and Universes.*

One of the areas where we are the most blocked is our beliefs about money. I have always been interested in finance, and over the past twenty-five years I have had the opportunity, both personally and professionally, to observe people and how they respond to the presence, or absence, of money.

According to the *Oxford Universal Dictionary,* the word *money* is derived from the Latin word "moneta," which was originally the name of a Roman goddess in whose temple money was coined. For thousands of years, money has been used as a medium of exchange and a measure of value. In its physical form, it is used to acquire goods and services, it is a common denominator for trade, and it serves as the foundation for a nation's economy. In its symbolic form, it is a measure for success, prestige, and power. When taken to excess, it is a tool for control.

Many people focus on money and all that it can buy as a barometer of their success in life. They think that if others see them as being successful, then they must be successful. They put all of their energies into the acquisition of money or possessions as a way of solving their inner problems, when in reality it doesn't solve a thing. It only masks it. Cut down the rainforests, pollute our oceans and soil, ravage the Earth of her gems and minerals. It doesn't matter if species are forced into extinction, if people are forced from their homes and die, if primary sources of food and protein are damaged or destroyed, forcing masses into starvation or a marginal existence. It doesn't matter if these actions are justified in the name of progress and improving the quality of one's life. Whose life? These unsustainable activities may make a few wealthy in the short term, but everyone poor in the long term. Once our natural resources are gone, we can't bring them back.

In the United States in the 1960s, the counterculture (i.e., hippies) broke away from this money-oriented society and swung to the opposite end of the spectrum, holding the belief—consciously or unconsciously—that money was filthy and corrupt (it represented the establishment) and that poverty was righteous and good. Unfortunately, this was not a healthy belief, either. Where our beliefs about money should move is to a balanced state wherein we can have money and we can embrace abundance without guilt, as long as its attainment does not harm another, as long as we can live sustainably on this Earth. According to Lester Brown of the Worldwatch Society, "A sustainable society is one that satisfies its needs without diminishing the prospects of future generations."[1] It is important for us to embrace money from the vantage point of sustainable abundance. It is also important for us to embrace, not denigrate, our own personal truth and integrity in regards to money. In this way, success and wealth, or the lack thereof, are defined by an inner, not an outer, statement of worth.

The Grateful Dead, both as an organization and as individuals, have come close to achieving this balanced state regarding money. Throughout their thirty-year history, the band members created their own style of music to please themselves, not others. Their goal was to discover new worlds through the evolution of their sound and to have fun doing it. It was not to make money, although money was eventually one of the results. As their income increased, so did their efforts to benefit social and environmental causes. Through the Rex Foundation, their nonprofit organization named after their road manager Rex Jackson, who died in 1976, they made 529 grants from 1992 to 1995 alone, totaling $4,083,212. Bob also has his own foundation, Further Foundation, from which he makes grants.

It is important that each and every one of us go within to release these areas of blocked energy in our lives and to become clear. When one is clear, one is in direct contact with the flow of the inner and outer worlds. One is free to express one's unique individuality as part of a whole, without fearing the loss of that individuality. One is free to express love, joy, happiness, and humor without fear of retaliation from pain, sadness, grief, and hate. These latter feelings will always exist on the Earth plane because various stages of mankind will still need to experience them as part of their growth in duality. However, each individual soul, once it has learned these lessons, needs to move on in order to continue in its growth, in its completion and wholeness, and eventually in its reunion with God.

All of you here on Earth are at different stages of spiritual growth, but those of you who have chosen to read my words and listen to my music have opened yourselves to the degree that you can now move freely forward into fully releasing your blocks—whatever they might be—and into freeing yourself, your world, and your Universe to move forward into the higher vibrations of love and consciousness, to become one with the God source, and to become truly free.

As you look at the stars in the night sky, ponder your

relationship with self and other. The light energy from the stars is there to support and encourage this process. They are your brothers and sisters in the Universe and send you much encouragement and love in the courageous process of learning and enlightenment that you have undertaken by being here on Earth at this time.

Standing under the night sky looking up at the stars used to make me very uncomfortable, and within minutes I would retreat back to the warmth and light of the house. It felt safe inside. I could see everything around me. I was in control.

As I started letting go of my inner structure and limiting beliefs, I gradually became more comfortable with the dark and the unknown. I first noticed this when I went outside to look at the beauty of the stars and realized that my relationship to them had shifted. They were no longer distant foreign objects in the sky, they were my friends. Then when the emotional pain in my life became too great, I would look up at the stars and secretly wish that I could go there, leaving the unhappiness I felt on Earth far behind. Distant memories would ripple the transparent veil that separated me from this other reality, and a sense of longing would rise up inside. Gazing at the night sky, I would think: Somewhere out there in the stars is my true home, where I am safe and happy and free. I want to go home.

Then one evening as I was looking up at the sky, I came to a sudden realization. My true home was not in the stars, it was not on Earth, it was within me. Now I understood. When I am comfortable and secure with who I am, I am comfortable and secure wherever I am.

The darkness need not be scary. When in the warm embrace of Nature, away from the craziness of the city, you can feel her dark, warm womb surround you and protect you. It is within this safety that you can continue your exploration of self and other.

Looking back at the star-studded heavens arching over me like the Egyptian goddess Nut, I knew that I was safe, both within the curve of her celestial body and the warmth of my own.[2]

We have spoken much, dear one, and we have spoken well. There is not much more. We will talk soon. Go in love. Go in peace.

WW: Thank you, Jerry. There is so much meaning and feeling in what you say that words cannot express it fully. Go in love. Go in peace.

Scarlet Begonias

Excerpt from lyrics by Robert Hunter

I ain't often right
but I've never been wrong
it seldom turns out the way
it does in the song
once in a while
you get shown the light
in the strangest of places
if you look at it right

MEDITATION

CHAPTER 19

Inner Knowing

WEDNESDAY, SEPTEMBER 13, 1995

IN MY MEDITATION, I FEEL JO HOVERING ABOVE ME. He is in a peaceful, quiet state. We mirror each other. This time I am the one to inquire if we can begin.

WW: Jer, are you ready yet?

JO: Yes, little one. I am now ready.

WW: Welcome.

JO: We shall begin.
    In the depths of our consciousness there is a space to which we can go that is the seat of all knowingness. This can be reached in meditation, in times of quiet and going within. Knowingness arises from the inside out. It is not based on learning or knowledge, although learning and knowledge

do help to open oneself up to get in touch with this know-ingness.

As you sit quietly in meditation, let your mind wander. Let it disengage. Then direct your focus inward to the light that lies in the solar plexus area. Visualize the light radiating forth from your core. Then follow that light inward and visualize that you are walking into a dark cave. Enter the cave. Feel your impressions. Ask your self (your higher self) how you should proceed inside this cave. Listen for the answer. It can come to you in words, feelings, or an undefined knowledge.

Follow this. If it says enter the darkness of the cave, then enter it. If you are to wait at the entrance, that is fine, too. Each time you meditate, in a quiet space without disruptions, go to the entrance of the cave, ask for higher guidance to heal you and guide you, then follow that guidance into the cave. The cave is your deeper knowingness, your place of oneness with the Universe, your connection to the web of life, the source of your true self, the gateway to freedom.

Or sometime in the peace and quiet, listen to beautiful, soul-filling music or chanting. Allow the sounds and melodies to take your mind away and act upon your inner vibrations, uninterrupted by the disturbances of the outside world. Listen to your feelings. See what issues or thoughts rise to the surface and address these issues. Do not ignore them or box them away. The music, the vision, is there to act as your guide to access the doors to your inner knowing, your deeper self.

You have been reading much, little one, about life in other realms. You have been discovering much, and you have found that the key to accessing and knowing all that exists in the Universe actually lies within. So often we first have to go out, to look at things, before realizing that the source of

*this knowledge has always been within us. We are a micro-
cosm of the macrocosm. The whole universe exists within us.
We need not look any further for our wisdom, our enlightenment, our true selves.*

Bob first expressed this concept to me years ago with the simple
statement "As above, so below." This belief originated in the
Hermetic or alchemical tradition, which describes a state in which
structures at one level of order mirror structures in another. This concept is now commonly accepted by our scientific community.

*Music is an incredible key to accessing this inner space.
So are the sounds of Nature. At first you may think them discordant, but that is because you are only able, with your
Earthly ears, to listen to the more obvious sounds: the song
of birds, the chirp of crickets, the wind whistling through the
trees. But what beautiful sounds do the trees themselves
make? What note does each blade of grass sing? What harmonies do the bushes add to the symphony that is Nature?
When you hear the complete creation, you will know the
beauty and soul-impact that the sounds of Nature have
upon you.*

In rare moments, I have heard this symphony of Nature. I am not
an auditory person, I am visual, so it is hard for me to hear sounds in
music or in Nature that other people can discern easily. It wasn't until
the last few years that the Dead played in concert that I could pick
out the rhythm of my brother's guitar from the rest of the instruments
(it helped when they changed the mix at the soundboard). People
used to tell me, "Wow, your brother sounded great! Wasn't that riff
of his in 'Sugar Magnolia' incredible?!" And I would reply enthusiastically, "Yeah, you're right!," knowing full well that I hadn't heard
it but also knowing that they had expected me to because (1) they had

heard it and (2) since I was Bob's sister, I must also be musical. Wrong on both counts. There have also been times when people have commented about Bob forgetting the lyrics or notes to a song, and I would reply seriously, "Yeah, you're right." I never lied. I just never let on.

Back to the symphony of Nature. The first time that I heard this was after I had returned home from one of Barbara Brennan's Healing Science Training Workshops. At the time I was doing some consulting work for her, coordinating and managing her workshops on the West Coast. I was still in an expanded state of awareness, which often lasted several days, and as I was walking my Irish setter, Jenny, through a grassy field late in the afternoon, I suddenly became aware of lots of noise. Shifting to my inner vision, I was surprised to discover that the sound came from the vegetation around me. I stopped and looked and listened. It was a beautiful symphony, with the voices of the plant kingdom acting as instruments. The tall dry grass waved its stalks in soprano, the large prickly thistles harmonized in alto while the dandelions chimed in brightly and the wildflowers added a beautiful melody.... The scattered green shrubs joined with tenor voices, the pine trees sounded in bass, and the swaying eucalyptus completed the arrangement in a deep baritone that came from the depths of their wide, old trunks. I couldn't believe it. The music lasted throughout my walk, but when I returned with Jenny the following morning, only a few notes were left for my ears. I have heard bits and pieces of this symphony of Nature since that time, but never again the full orchestra.

Do not hurry so. Do not fill your day with doingness. Take time for yourself. Time to be alone with the quiet. Time to be. Meditate. See. Listen. Open yourself up to the energies of life, of spirit, that surround and support you during your time on this Earth plane.

Yes, times are changing rapidly. Yes, there is much need

for mankind to change its ways of negativity, but first you must find the knowingness within you. You must see your fears and release them. You must become very clear in order for you to come in touch with your life's plan and in order for you to have the knowingness to fulfill it. This plan will be to help the Earth, help mankind, and help the Universe. Each of us has our own unique purpose. Get in touch with it, and in doing so you will raise your vibrations, which will change the world.

As the Earth Mother once said to me in the small cave outside Sedona: "You must heal yourself first before you can heal me. In healing yourself, you heal me."

The power to help, to change that which needs changing, lies within and flows out. Once you get in touch with this true source, your true self, miracles can happen (as they do every day). Only this time you will recognize these miracles as being a normal part of life; you were just not aware of them before.

Be in peace, dear one. Be in love. Tomorrow will be our last "formal" session. The message I have to deliver will be complete and we can continue with the next section of our work together.

WW: Thank you, Jerry. Go in peace. Go in love.

Eyes of the World

Excerpt from lyrics by Robert Hunter

there comes a redeemer
and he slowly, too, fades away
there follows a wagon behind him
that's loaded with clay
and the seeds that were silent
all burst into bloom and decay
the night comes so quiet
and it's close on the heels of the day

sometimes we live no
particular way but our own
sometimes we visit your country
and live in your home
sometimes we ride on your horses
sometimes we walk alone
sometimes the songs that we hear
are just songs of our own

wake up to find out
that you are the eyes of the world
but the heart has its beaches
its homeland and thoughts
of its own
wake now, discover that
you are the song that
the morning brings
but the heart has its seasons
its evenings
and songs of its own

THREAD OF LIGHT

CHAPTER 20

One

tHURSDay, septeMBeR 14, 1995

SILENCE. PEACE. MEDITATION. I OPEN MY CHANNEL
to JO.

WW: Dear Jerry, do you wish to speak today?

A flow of radiant golden energy surrounds his light body. He is in
a state of deep peace, unconditional love. A sense of well-being
enfolds me.

JO: Yes, dear one.
Unconditional love. Peace. Well-being. This is the state
for which we must strive on Earth, but which is more read-
ily available to us in the higher dimensions.
You had some questions, little sister. The first is how
to explain my presence to those who read what has been
written.

I feel a slight shock. Yes, I did have questions. Ever since I started communicating with JO, I wondered how I was going to explain what was happening to those who read these communications, but I had never asked him directly. I had only thought this silently to myself. I am also surprised that the mental, practical part of me still feels a jolt when my thoughts are read so clearly. It is a reminder to me that thoughts have their own energy, whether or not they are verbally expressed, and that they can be received telepathically by anyone who has the ability and the desire to hear them.

> *I will try to offer a simple image. Imagine a line or thread of brilliant light radiating from the God source. This light is the oversoul, which has separated from God in order to experience self. At this level, the oversoul is not influenced by the Earth's electromagnetic field. However, as this light, which vibrates at a very pure, high frequency, enters the Earth's atmosphere during the process of reincarnation, it is weighed down by the Earth's strong, dense electromagnetic field, which lowers its frequency to the point where it manifests physically. There can be multiple aspects or threads of the oversoul incarnate at the same time. One of my threads of light became the being Jerry Garcia. Jerry, I (his oversoul), and God are always connected. This link can never be broken. Do you now understand?*
>
> *Your second question was how to explain our ability to communicate with each other. In order for us to transmit and receive this information, it has been necessary for our frequencies to match. Because you already vibrate at a very high frequency and are familiar with both the Earth and higher realms, the link or bond between us was able to be made. Be clear, though, this link was made by mutual agreement between the two of us long ago before you incarnated. I can-*

not link with you, or you with me, if either of us did not
wish it so.

Your third question was why you could not connect with
Jerry's spirit in the astral. At this time, it is not possible to
connect to the spirit that was Jerry on Earth. He is on an
astral level that cannot be penetrated by linking. It is a high-
frequency level of light surrounding the upper reaches of the
Earth, which some call the Light Network. It is like a super-
highway of energy that holds both intelligence and information. Here the spirit of many famous Earth beings, both alive
and dead, reside because this is where their energies can circulate around the planet and reach the greatest number of
people. This is not necessarily an idyllic place, however, for
either the being or those the being touches.

Your final question was why so many people who knew
Jerry and his work felt such intense pain and grief at his passing. If the being at the level of the Light Network embraces
his true self and honors all that he is able to do for others,
then he is in a high state of peace, love, and grace, and those
who are energetically connected with him feel this enlightened state within themselves to the best of their abilities.
However, if the being, such as Jerry, does not honor his true
self, does not inwardly acknowledge the contributions that
he has rightfully given to mankind, and does not complete
his mission on Earth, then he experiences grief and regret at
this level and these feelings are likewise picked up by those
in contact with him.

The grief that so many felt in Jerry's passing is partially
the grief that they were picking up from him. It was also
their own grief in losing one they looked at as a beloved
leader, and grief within themselves for having to let go of a
way of life, and change, and grow.

The grief that so many experienced also served to bind each one closer to the other. Bonds have been strengthened and a new light is emerging to lead them forward on their path. This light is radiant. It is pure. It is sacred. It expresses love and joy. It honors self and other. It is highly and clearly connected to the God source. It is not a leader because leaders for those to follow are not needed in this coming age. What is needed is for each person, each being, to honor who he or she truly is and to become his or her own leader, working in community with others.

Understand, please, that we each have our own individual personalities that exist throughout eternity. We learn, we grow, but we are always uniquely ourselves. When we merge with other in community, we do not lose this individuality. We voluntarily merge it with other and thereby create a greater whole in which we grow as individuals and we grow as part of a whole.

It is important, in this transition of times, to place no one above you. **DO NOT GIVE YOUR POWER AWAY.** *No one can take it from you. Only you can dispense it. Do not do this. Keep your power within you, within your core, and move forward in the world from this center, which is the true you, the true self. When you are connected on Earth with this true self, then you are consciously connected with your oversoul and you are consciously connected with God. Remember, the thread of light, the line of energy, that runs from the God source to you is and always will be fully functioning and complete. You are one with all of life. You are one with the Universe. You are one with All That Is. You are ONE.*

Jerry, while on the Earth plane and now in the spirit, is helping you get to this point. Now another will lead you for-

*ward. Do not search for him. Do not set him apart from you
or above you. He is you. Each and every one of you.*

*Honor your self, love your self, and in honoring and lov-
ing self, you will be able to honor and love other. The path
is always an inward path, but once the depths have been
reached and the core which is you embraced, then your light
energy can be released outward to positively influence
friends, family, people you brush by on the street, and beings
from other worlds.*

*You will no longer believe in the illusion of duality. You
will know your self to be a part of the whole. The changes
that go on within will create a change, a shift, in the lines of
light that connect you to others. And as they change, their
changes will likewise influence you. Be careful what you
think, what you do, what you put out there, because no
energy is ever lost in the Universe. Your thoughts, your
actions, will continue to influence others once you have
released them.*

*It is time for me to go now. My work with you is coming
to completion and soon Jerry's spirit will be free to rejoin me
at the higher frequency. Know I speak the truth. Know I
speak with love for all of you. Listen to the music. It sings
within each of us and lights our way.*

*Go in love. Go in peace. We are all connected. We are
one, for eternity.*

*WW: Thank you, dear one. Your words strike deeply within
me. Go in love. Go in peace.*

I am in a state of bliss, yet sad. Over the past five weeks, our energies
have grown and blended together. I have absorbed some of JO's
higher essence and he has absorbed an experience of me. I look

around and feel unconditional love for all of life. A smile envelops my face and I am graced with the return of innocence. I am also pleased with all that we have accomplished and deeply grateful for all that we have shared. The "formal" sessions with JO are now over and I will wait for him to contact me as he said he would.

Uncle John's Band

Excerpt from lyrics by Robert Hunter

well, the first days are the hardest days,
don't you worry anymore
when life looks like easy street
there is danger at your door
think this through with me
let me know your mind
whoa-oh, what i want to know,
is are you kind?

MY SPIRIT WOLVES, OR'U AND SNOWBALL

Shadow

fRIDay, septeMBeR 15, 1995

IT IS NIGHTTIME. I AM SLEEPING PEACEFULLY, STILL blissed-out from my final session with JO the previous day. Gradually I sense a shift within my energy field. Someone, something, has entered the dark recesses of my dream and I feel uneasy. Becoming more alert, I look around and catch a stealthy movement outlined against the walls of my subconscious. A black enshrouded figure silently approaches. It is stalking me. How can this be? Where did it come from? The intuitive part of me feels threatened and fearful, but my rational mind thinks: Don't worry. Nothing will happen. It's only a dream.

As the echo of my thoughts drifts away, the shadow form suddenly strikes, trying to capture me in its evil embrace. Instinctively I strike back, throwing up wards of impenetrable energy and calling in my spirit wolves for protection. There is a bright flash, then shields of transparent light encircle me and two snarling wolves are crouched on either side of my body, ready to attack.

The evil presence draws back momentarily to consider this new situation, then quietly, calmly, it turns around and glides back into the darkness from which it had come. As it disappears from my awareness, I can feel the taint of its corrosive energy coursing through my blood.

A heated anger rises up within me, anger more at myself than at the shadow form. I know dream walkers exist, and I know some use their powers for good and some for evil. How could I have become so complacent? From the center of my dreamscape, I scream: "Why was I attacked? Who did this to me?" But there is no answer, only silence. All is quiet once more.

Before reentering the depths of sleep, I double-check the safety of my wards and station my spirit wolves nearby. One lies down next to my bed and the other moves to guard the bedroom door. Knowing they will warn me if the shadow form returns, I slip gradually back into a dreamless state.

Rays from the rising sun slowly awaken me and I roll over, opening my eyes and shifting my gaze. The wolf by my bed is sleeping calmly. The other one is sitting in the doorway facing the front door and watching attentively. As I get up, I feel a surge of anger and the taint of evil pulsing through my veins and the reality of my dream crashes back into my consciousness. I have been unjustly attacked! Everything had been so nice and peaceful and now this. Not knowing where else to go in my anguish and confusion, I decide to contact JO. I know he had said that he would contact me, but I must understand what happened so I can rid myself of this awful feeling.

Sitting in my chair in the living room, I try to quiet my disturbed mind and clear my disrupted energy field, but a fearful splinter of last night's dream remains. I ignore it and push on, raising my frequency and settling into my familiar state of meditation. The splinter soon dissolves, and when I am centered and peaceful, I reach out to JO.

WW: Jerry, will you speak with me today?

JO: Yes, I will, but we are done with the sessions.

Without me saying another word, he starts to answer the questions that had been raging through my mind.

Today I wish to speak to you about your own personal life. The being that came to you last night, that you did not like, was there to teach you. This is a different kind of teacher that we have in the higher realms. This type of teacher vibrates at a very high rate, is very clear, and acts as a reflection of what you need to look at. He will not harm you, although if that is what you need and you request that experience, even on an unconscious level, he will honor your request. He is there to teach you about the shadow side.

In working with me, you had become full of the positive, clear vibrations that are felt in dealing at these levels. You had forgotten about the shadow, the dark side. It is all around and within you. It exists whether you see it or not.

Do not become complacent. Be on guard. Be aware. You will not be caught by surprise then as you were last night.

Often we must test our strength and courage in order to see more clearly our weaknesses. You responded well, although the anger was a little more than necessary, and you felt the taint that the dark side leaves in your being.

Be open to all aspects of yourself. Explore them. See how your shadow defines your light. Look within and find balance. Do not be fearful. No harm will come to you as long as you do not become complacent.

This is all I wish to say to you this morning. You may release your wolves until the next time you need them. We will talk again tomorrow.

We did not talk the following day or on the days to follow. Although I still meditated and checked in regularly with JO, he did not choose to come forth. I went on with my day-to-day life and soon became fully absorbed in handling the changes taking place in it, changes involving my work, my personal relationships, and, most of all, my inner self. Eventually I even stopped checking in with JO. I knew that he would contact me again as he had said, but it would be when he (not I) was ready.

book two

1 9 9 6

JULY 10–AUGUST 11

Crazy Fingers

Excerpt from lyrics by Robert Hunter

so swift and bright
strange figures of light
float in air

who can stop what must arrive now?
something new is waiting to be born

TALKING SYMBOLS[1]

Problems

WEDNESDAY, JULY 10, 1996

THE PHONE RINGS. I'VE JUST FINISHED DINNER AND am in the middle of doing dishes.

I pick up the receiver and say hello in a somewhat preoccupied voice.

"Hi, it's me," the voice on the other end replies.

It's Bob. I'm surprised to hear from him because he's out on the Further Festival tour with Ratdog. I vaguely recall that he was playing New Jersey tonight because I had made arrangements for friends in New York to go see him. The show must have just ended.

"How's it going?" I ask.

"Okay," he says, his voice showing a hint of concern. "But I keep getting this feeling that something is wrong with Jerry and he wants me to help. Can you check in on him for me? I'm leaving in a few minutes on the bus, so you can leave the message on my home phone and I'll pick it up the next chance I get."

"Okay," I reply. "I'll do it in the morning and will let you know."

I reflect about my last contact with Jerry's Oversoul. It has been ten months. So much has happened since we last talked. Then I remember that JO had said there was going to be more work to do together.

Early the next morning, I go back to my old routine. I sit peacefully in my chair, meditate, and raise my energy. When I'm ready, I test my connection with JO.

WW: Jerry, are you there?

JO: Yes, I'm ready to talk when you are.

WW: Okay, let's go.

JO: Jerry's spirit is having problems leaving the level of the astral plane where he is currently resting. Bob has asked if he can help. He can.

WW: How can Bob help?

JO: The music he is playing is good, but he needs to raise his vibration higher so that he can connect better with Jerry's astral vibration. He can do this in meditation. Once he gets the higher vibrational connection with Jerry, the path will remain and he can tune in to it with his intent, then relax and go with it.

The purpose here is somewhat complex, so let me explain. Since Jerry is no longer in the physical, he does not have direct access to the Earth energy and human energy that used to surround and support him. It is this energy that he needs, however, to give himself, shall we say, the boost to move out of his current plane and into a higher one. He still has much processing to do in the astral, but the astral has many layers and it is time for Jerry to move up. His purpose on Earth is not fulfilled and so his tenure in the astral will still be for some time, but he is stuck and needs to move within that dimension.

Bob, by creating a high vibrational link with Jerry, will act as a clear (and I emphasize the need to be clear) conduit for the Earth energies and human energies that are so highly focused at him during his concert. These energies enter Bob and currently stay there, within. However, once the link is established, they will enter Bob and flow through him, up the path of the link to Jerry. Jerry will then be able to use these energies to raise the vibration of his astral body and move up to the next level.

We had hoped that Jerry would have had the strength to do this himself, but the damage done to his physical body during this last incarnation has affected his energy level, and until he is out of the density and pull of the astral dimension, he will continue to need and use Bob's help.

Do not misunderstand, there are many ways in which Bob and Jerry are working together. However, this is a specific need that must be addressed at this time in order for Jerry to fulfill his mission on Earth.

Is this clear, little one?

WW: Yes, thank you. I'll let Bob know, and if there are further questions, I'll get back to you.

JO: That is good, and when you talk with your brother, please ask him to listen to us. Our communication is clear up to the point of being translated into his consciousness, and then the damage to his circuitry that occurred previously in his life from drugs interferes.

When those in the higher dimensions, such as JO, communicate with us on Earth, it is often done through subconscious contact. This type of communication has a more dreamlike, less tangible quality and relies on symbols to transmit meaning. These symbols are received by our brain, where they are translated, to the best extent possible, into conscious words and expressions. The clearer we are, the higher vibration we have, the easier it is to receive and comprehend this information.

Ask him to drink more mineral water. That will help to repair the synapses so that he can receive and process our vibrations more clearly and easily.

WW: I'll do that. Anything else?

JO: No, that is all, little sister. We will talk again soon.

After coming out of meditation, I dial Bob's number and leave the information for him on his voice mail. He picks it up the following day.

Cosmic Charley

Excerpt from lyrics by Robert Hunter

say you'll come back when you can
whenever your airplane happens to land
maybe i'll be back here, too
it all depends on what's with you

new ones comin' as the old ones go
everything's movin' here but much too slowly
little bit quicker and we might have time
to say, "how do you do?" before we're left behind

MANDALA OF ONE

Shoreline

t u e s D a y ,   j u L y   3 0 ,   1 9 9 6

THE FURTHER FESTIVAL IS BEING HELD AT THE SHORE-
line Amphitheater in Mountain View, about forty-five miles south of
San Francisco. Of the original Grateful Dead band members, Bob
and Mickey Hart are performing with their own bands. Bruce
Hornsby, who joined the Dead on keyboard after Brent Mydland
died and before Vince Welnick was hired, is playing with his band.
And rumors have it that Phil Lesh, the Dead's bass guitarist, will be
jamming with them.

This is home territory for the Dead. It is also ten days before the
first anniversary of Jerry Garcia's death. The Grateful Dead had
played Shoreline often and we used to say jokingly that they were the
house band. Bill Graham, along with his company, Bill Graham
Presents, was the West Coast promoter for the band and the creator
of the amphitheater. Seen from the air, the complex is in the shape of
the Dead's Steal Your Face skull-and-lightning-bolt icon.

Because there are so many bands and acts performing on the tour,
the show starts in midafternoon. Bob and his band, Ratdog, are

scheduled to be the last group to perform, around nine-thirty P.M., followed by a jam of all the artists. The show is scheduled to end at eleven P.M.

It is a beautiful, warm summer's day and we are blessed that there is no chilly fog hanging over the distant hills, poised to pour in. I arrive around four P.M., after the first few sets are over. As I drive into the backstage parking lot, everything looks like a Grateful Dead concert. Brightly colored banners wave lazily in the breeze. A kaleidoscope of blue, green, yellow, red, and orange tie-dyed Deadheads circulate about, standing in line waiting to get in, hanging out with friends, or just passing by with one finger raised high in the air, waiting for a miracle (a free ticket). It is a festive, joyous atmosphere and the energy is high. Everyone has missed the music, and this adds to their anticipation of an incredible show. But the feeling has changed: Jerry is gone and the Dead are not playing.

As I walk to the backstage dressing rooms, I see Phil Lesh and his wife, Jill, standing in the patio area. They are laughing and talking to friends as I go over to say hello. Not only have we all missed the music and seeing one another, but the band members have missed playing together.

I stop by Bob's dressing room to drop off my purse and jacket. It is still early and he has not arrived yet. Then I join a friend and we head out to our seats, walking around the backstage basketball court where some of the stage crew are playing a quick game, up the stairs, past the backstage beer garden, and out into the crowd. This is going to be a totally new experience for me. During a Dead show, I would never sit for very long in the audience because I always had things to do (not to mention being claustrophobic). Usually I could be found backstage running around, meeting and greeting people, doing business, visiting with old friends, or just hiding out in Bob's room away from the pounding vibration of the speakers. Strange as it seems, at best I only saw a part of each show. Today, however, I decide that it is a new beginning and I will discover a bit of what everyone else has been experiencing for the past thirty years. I will stay in the audience from the beginning of the Ratdog performance to the end of the show.

We relax in our seats and listen to the music. Each band plays its own songs plus one or two Grateful Dead songs. In between some of the sets, I get up and walk through the Mall, a vast assortment of merchandise booths and food concessions on the upper level of the concert site. Here you can buy anything mystical, magical, hippie-ish, or Dead-esque. It is the same group of merry merchants who frequented all of the Dead shows at Shoreline, and people are enjoying browsing and buying items that they have a hard time finding anywhere else.

As the afternoon drifts into evening and dusk starts to descend gently upon us, I become aware of magic building all around. Looking about from my seat, I sense the vibration of the audience and the rhythm of the music begin to rise and flow, blending with one another like brilliant colors of light poured into a clear pool of sound and swirled together with an invisible wand creating a rainbow of spiraling energy.

Then I shift my vision to a vantage point miles above the ground and gaze down through the airplane window of my mind's eye. Like a Grateful Dead concert, this one appears to me as a pinpoint of intense gold-white light that radiates out in a circular fan formation into the Earth and out to the Universe. And as it was at a Grateful Dead concert, this light contains the energies of the band, the music, and the audience, which are transmitted out to many realms.

Bruce Hornsby and Mickey Hart have finished playing with their bands and Bob is now onstage with Ratdog. They are more than halfway through the set and everyone is up, standing in front of their seats or on the back lawn, swirling and dancing to the music, each in his or her own ecstatic way. Bob is having a great time, too. He is playfully present in each note, and one with the Muses, who sing in harmony with his voice and the sound of his guitar.

Bruce joins Bob onstage and the first few chords of "Cassidy" rise from the speakers to greet us in a familiar melody. As my body starts swinging to its rhythm, I am surprised to feel a shift in consciousness. The lights take on a shimmering luminosity and the musical vibrations penetrate deeper into my body. Spirit has joined me, signaling that something important is about to happen. I wonder what it is, and in reply a thought enters my mind: Tonight is the night that we are going to free Jerry.

I switch my attention and tune in to him on the astral plane. His energy is extremely heavy, weighted down by the soul memories of pain and the damage of addiction that had clogged his body on Earth. I can feel his instinctive desire to move on, blanketed by the frustration of his inability to do so. He is like Houdini, wrapped in chains and locked into a straitjacket of his own creation, but unlike Houdini, he doesn't have the strength to escape on his own. He feels the probing fingers of my thoughts and flashes a thankful spark of hope and acknowledgment back to me, but still he cannot speak.

In the background of my awareness I hear Rob Wasserman's bass solo come to an end as the rest of the band joins him onstage. They pick up his beat and move easily into "Easy Answers." As the rhythm of the music builds, I remember what JO had said and focus on Bob. With the graceful mudra-movements of my hands, I spontaneously start to gather his heightened energy. When it is condensed into a tight iridescent ball of light, I project it up to Jerry with the thrust of my right arm. Then I look. It reaches him but nothing happens. The light is absorbed into his energy field and dissipates. Why? Words from the song reach my ears and I have to smile. They're right. There is no "easy answer." I will try again using more power.

In order to do this, I tune in telepathically with Bob. This time instead of working with the energy he is projecting, I ask him to join forces with me. It is like building a bridge. Before you can string the cables to safely suspend the heavy weight of the roadway and traffic, you must construct two strong towers for support. Bob and I are the towers, the band members are the cables, our energetic connection is the roadway, and the traffic is the increased power that flows over it.

I know from experience that the set is drawing to a close and there isn't much time. Bob starts a rousing rendition of "Josephine" as I refocus my attention and intensify my effort. Gradually I begin to gather the energy, first from Bob and myself until our foundations are strong and solid, then from the band and the vibration of their music. With each movement of my hands, I draw and consolidate more and more of their energy with Bob's and mine, condensing its rising frequency into a radiant ball until I feel that it is powerful enough. Then I wait until the song reaches its crescendo to give me added strength, and with the full force of my body I project its light up to Jerry. And watch. And wait.

When it hits, I see a sharp shift in his energy field as if he was struck by a bolt of lightning. The jolt loosens the binding of his chains, but instead of them snapping off to set him free, their hold remains and his expanded form is jerked down, hurling the energy wave that I had sent back to me with increased force. When it hits, I feel crushed beneath its enormous weight and an overwhelming sense of hopelessness floods through me, washing waves of despair into every cell of my body. For a moment, I am afraid that Jerry's heaviness will be too great to shift, but I know that a negative thought like this can be self-defeating, so I banish it from my mind and replace it with the confidence of success.

There is a break in the music as Mickey Hart, Phil Lesh, and the other artists join Bob onstage to jam. I stand still, breathing deeply and gathering the last remnants of my strength. I check within. The possibility of failure does not exist. Looking up at the star-studded sky, I send my plea through our galaxy into the dark-embracing void. I call out to All That Is, to my spirit guides, to all who wish to help with their highest love and support, then I lower my gaze to the bright starlights of the stage as the first notes of "Truckin'" dance from my brother's guitar. I laugh quietly to myself. Through the music I have once again received my answer. I have to "keep on truckin.'"

The frequency of the music starts to build, enfolding the audience within the grasp of its vibration. I quickly reconnect with Bob, then together we connect with the other band members onstage, focusing especially on Phil, Mickey, and Bruce because of their strong heart-link with Jerry. Then without thinking I intuitively connect with the dancing, throbbing energy of the audience. Staying firmly centered within myself, I carefully weave all of the energies together, creating a brightly colored fabric of great strength and beauty. Observing my unconscious movements with my consciousness, I suddenly understand why I had failed. It was not just the band, it was not just the music, it was not just the audience that made the Grateful Dead experience so incredibly powerful. It was the individual parts blending together as one, and only with this power of ONE can Jerry be freed.

"Truckin'" ends and the musicians move seamlessly into "The Other One." Moving wildly to the music, an individual yet a part of the whole, I gather more and more energy together with the mudras of my hands. Like a swirling whirlpool, the energies on the outside are drawn into the magnetism of the middle, increasing in intensity and power as they spiral deeper and deeper, tighter and tighter, until they form a bright sphere of pure radiating light in the center. Revived by the love and support of all present, strengthened by the transcendent beat of the music, I gather this pure ball of light in my hands, and with one final thrust I cast it directly up to Jerry. When it hits, the intensity of its high vibration jars his astral body loose, snapping the chains and catapulting him up to the next level. I am ecstatic, jumping up and down to the music and silently yelling: We did it! We did it! Then I stop to feel how he is doing. The heaviness and constraint are gone and he is sleeping peacefully, healing and adjusting to the higher, clearer frequency of this plane. I shift my gaze and look around the amphitheater, not at the people but at those beings who assisted from the spirit realm. They are hovering above the scene, rejoicing and applauding our success, our success as ONE.

Still in an altered state, I pick the beat back up and move gently to its rhythm. The motion helps to ground me so that I can carefully lower the heightened energies that I had used and integrate them safely into both the physical dimension and into my body. When the song ends, my movement stops. I breathe a sigh of relief and relax. The musicians move into their encore, the Jefferson Airplane's Sixties hit "White Rabbit," but my thoughts are still with Jerry. I leave my seat, moving past the dancing, singing people, and weave my way backstage, where I enter Bob's dressing room and sit down on the couch, exhausted. Not wanting to stay too late after the show because I will be leaving early in the morning for the mountains, I decide to tell Bob briefly what happened when he gets offstage, saving the details until I return and we can find time to sit quietly together.

Standing on the Moon

Excerpt from lyrics by Robert Hunter

STANDING ON THE MOON
I SEE A SHADOW ON THE SUN
STANDING ON THE MOON
THE STARS GO FADING ONE BY ONE
I HEAR A CRY OF VICTORY
AND ANOTHER OF DEFEAT
A SCRAP OF AGE-OLD LULLABY
DOWN SOME FORGOTTEN STREET

STANDING ON THE MOON
WHERE TALK IS CHEAP AND VISION TRUE
STANDING ON THE MOON
BUT I WOULD RATHER BE WITH YOU
SOMEWHERE IN SAN FRANCISCO
ON A BACK PORCH IN JULY
JUST LOOKING UP TO HEAVEN
AT THIS CRESCENT IN THE SKY

IN REMEMBRANCE

First Anniversary

tHURSDay, auGUSt 8, 1996

SITTING ON A LOG IN FRONT OF A LARGE FIRE
beneath the tall pine trees of the Sierra Nevada, I look up at the
crystal-clear stars sparkling in the velvet-black sky. They remind me
of the stars I had seen at Shoreline the week before, and my thoughts
wander back to that evening. Since then, I have slept well and
awoken each morning to the fragrance of fresh mountain air. My days
have been filled with hiking, horseback riding, swimming, and boat-
ing; my nights with conversation and reading. Several nights we took
turns reading fairy tales out loud while roasting marshmallows in the
fireplace. During this time, I have checked in regularly with Jerry's
spirit and found he was still sleeping peacefully on the higher astral
level. All was well in both of our worlds, except for tonight. Tonight
a feeling of loss and sadness nudges at my contentment. It is the eve
of Jerry's death one year ago and I miss him.

The heat of day evaporated into the chill of evening a while ago
but I did not notice. A movement at the west end of the fire brings
me back to attention and I edge closer to the flames, seeking warmth.

One of my friends has just placed a broken pine branch wrapped with beautiful wildflowers and grass from the meadow upright in the soft, moist earth. I look at him and ask what it means. He tells me that when he was gathering firewood, an unusual feeling came over him and he felt that he should create this offering in honor of Jerry. He didn't know why—he never knew Jerry and had been to only a few Grateful Dead shows in his whole life. I look back at the flames. As they crackle and dance toward the sky, their shadows caress the offering branch and bring it to life. I know that Jerry's spirit is with us, as it is with many others this night.

A few minutes later, our other friends join us, taking places randomly around the fire. Staring into the flames, we enter into a state of silence like monks meditating in the cathedral of Nature. Almost out of habit, I check on Jerry in the astral, and much to my surprise, instead of seeing him in a resting state, I find he is up and moving about easily. Clothed in a floor-length cotton-white robe girded at the waist by a thick white cord, he appears healthy and happy, yet his features are slightly different from the ones he had on Earth. His thirty-ish face is smooth and beardless, his wavy brown hair softly touches the top of his collar, his body is slender, his hands are whole, and his vision clear. A part of me expects to see large white wings sprouting from his back, but none are visible. My thoughts touch his awareness and he turns his attention toward me. A joyous voice reaches out.

J: Hey, little sis, we did it! I'M FREE!

I have learned to be cautious when dealing with spirit, so I reply questioningly.

WW: Jerry, is this you? You can communicate now?

J: Yeah, isn't it great! Now we can really get going!

Wanting to make sure that I had the right connection, I check in with his oversoul for verification. Yes, JO confirms, I am talking to Jerry's spirit in the astral. On the anniversary of his death, the healing force of all the loving thoughts and prayers that people are projecting to him, the private ceremonies in his honor, have awakened him into the light. Despite my joy at finally being able to talk with him in his astral body, I deeply miss talking with him in his physical one. It's just not the same. There is a void in me that can't be filled with memories and visions.

A sense of sadness and loss fills my heart. Jerry feels this sadness and in response he comforts me with waves of unconditional love and gratitude. With all of us working together, he is free at last to join us in the spirit and complete his mission on Earth. We have helped him do this and now, as "the grateful dead," he is ready to help us in return.

Franklin's Tower

Excerpt from lyrics by Robert Hunter

IN ANOTHER TIME'S FORGOTTEN SPACE
YOUR EYES LOOKED FROM YOUR MOTHER'S FACE
WILDFLOWER SEED ON THE SAND AND STONE
MAY THE FOUR WINDS BLOW YOU SAFELY HOME

YOU ASK ME WHERE THE FOUR WINDS DWELL
IN FRANKLIN'S TOWER THERE HANGS A BELL
IT CAN RING, TURN NIGHT TO DAY
RING LIKE FIRE WHEN YOU LOSE YOUR WAY

GOD HELP THE CHILD WHO RINGS THAT BELL
IT MAY HAVE ONE GOOD RING LEFT, YOU CAN'T TELL
ONE WATCH BY NIGHT, ONE WATCH BY DAY
IF YOU GET CONFUSED, JUST LISTEN TO THE MUSIC PLAY

SOME COME TO LAUGH THEIR PAST AWAY
SOME COME TO MAKE IT JUST ONE MORE DAY
WHICHEVER WAY YOUR PLEASURE TENDS
IF YOU PLANT ICE, YOU'RE GONNA HARVEST WIND

IN FRANKLIN'S TOWER THE FOUR WINDS SLEEP
LIKE FOUR LEAN HOUNDS THE LIGHTHOUSE KEEP
WILDFLOWER SEED IN THE SAND AND WIND
MAY THE FOUR WINDS BLOW YOU HOME AGAIN

ROLL AWAY THE DEW
ROLL AWAY THE DEW
ROLL AWAY THE DEW
YOU BETTER ROLL AWAY THE DEW

IN THE SPIRIT

CHAPTER 25

A Tale Is Told

SUNDAY, AUGUST 11, 1996

IT IS FIVE FORTY-FIVE A.M., THE DAWN OF A NEW DAY
in the mountains. I look out the window. Drops of dew decorate the
plants and wildflowers, reflecting the morning light as it climbs up
through the trees. It is our last day here. Lying back peacefully in bed,
I tuck the blankets beneath my chin and let my mind wander, thinking of all the things that need to be done. Out of habit I check in
casually, almost absentmindedly, with Jerry. I am still testing the connection, and all that we have done so far is exchange pleasantries.

Much to my surprise, he is right there, loud and clear, full of
energy and ready to go. I'm not prepared for this, so in the midst of
my confusion all I can say is:

WW: Hi, Jer.

He replies enthusiastically:

*J: Hi, little sis. It's time for you to write a tale about the
Grateful Dead.*

WW: Now? It's five forty-five in the morning!

Then I think irritably to myself: Just because he's up and awake all the time now doesn't mean that I have to be. Jerry hears my thought but chooses to ignore it.

J: I'm ready when you are.

No! This is not what I had in mind to do at this hour. I am about to tell Jerry that I want to wait until it is more convenient and I can fully focus on what he is saying, when a little voice in the back of my head jumps up and chatters wildly: "Uh-oh. The last time you said no to spirit, the smoke alarm went off in your bedroom. Are you sure you want to do that?" I sure don't. That would be even worse, so I quickly change my mind and resignedly tell Jerry:

WW: Just a minute. Let me get up and find some paper and a pen, then we'll see what happens.

Quietly I find what I need and return to bed. Taking my time, I prop myself up with pillows next to the window, pull the blanket over my legs, place a book under the paper, and adjust the pen in my hand. I look around the cabin. Everyone is sleeping soundly. Only the birds outside and I are awake, greeting the dawn. A familiar fear creeps briefly into my mind and I wonder if I will be able to channel the information. Then I relax and smile. There is only one way to find out.

WW: Okay, Jerry, I'm ready when you are.

And so the tale begins.

A Tale of the Dead

ONCE UPON A TIME, AS WE UNDERSTAND TIME, there lived five young musicians in a beautiful land near the sea. The first musician, whose name was Jerry, was a fine artist who taught guitar for a living while he went to school. The second musician, whose name was Bobby, also went to school. He loved playing his guitar so much that he carried it with him everywhere. Bobby and Jerry played together at the local music store whenever they could. They were soon joined by Billy, the drummer, Pigpen, the keyboardist, and Phil, the bass guitarist.

Each one had amazing talents, and when they played together, new and wondrous sounds came forth, so it wasn't long before they decided to form a band. At first it was a jug band, but that soon evolved into a rock and roll band called the Warlocks, for they knew deep inside that they were more than just ordinary musicians. Then one day they heard that there were other musicians in a far-off land who also called themselves the Warlocks, so they decided to change their name.

Now, names have magical powers, and the band members wanted a name that represented who they truly were and that would give greater meaning to the cosmic music that they played. When people heard this music, they became transported into magnificent worlds of color and sound and dancing and love. The music would swirl around them and through them, lifting them up and away to mystical places within themselves.

Jerry, Bobby, Billy, Pigpen, and Phil came up with many names, but none felt right. Then one day, Jerry was reading an old folktale from a distant land. It was about the grateful dead. "That's it," he said. "We will call ourselves the Grateful Dead, for we, too, travel beyond this world with our music and help people who are in need, not a need for money, but a need to walk the path within themselves to find the freedom and love that lies deep inside."

All the members of the band rejoiced, for at last they had found a name, a powerful, magical name, that would help them speak to the people as they traveled and played, that would open doors for them into darker areas of their lives where they could find the light.

Time passed, as we understand time, and a sixth musician joined the band. His name was Mickey and he played percussion instruments of all kinds.

The Dead moved from the countryside into a big city, where they played with other amazing musicians. A whole culture grew up, of which they were a part, that placed value on love and peace instead of fear and war, that broke away from the strict standards of society and created its own standards, which were much more open and tolerant and creative. The band's music grew and evolved as its members grew and evolved, and as the people around them grew and evolved, and as society and the world grew and evolved. The music set the beat and opened the path for all to follow who liked adventure and new discoveries.

Time passed, as we understand time, and Pigpen died, as we understand death, and Keith took his place in the band.

Time passed, as we understand time, and Keith died, as we understand death, and Brent took his place in the band.

Time passed, as we understand time, and Brent died, as we understand death, and Vince took his place in the band.

By now, the Grateful Dead were known far and wide, from the great pyramids of Egypt to the courts of Europe to the lands of many native people. Their music wove a wondrous spell around all who heard it and brought each and every one together into a large family, a family based not upon birth into the physical but upon birth into the light.

And so it seemed that all was well. The members of the band, like many of the people who listened to their music, had experienced the pain of loss, the devastation of drugs, and the struggle of addiction. They had moved forward through dark passages and passed through doors that led to a deeper respect for their physical and emotional bodies, the value of their lives, the beauty of their feelings, and the joy of their spirits.

But all was not well, and it came to pass one day that Jerry could no longer stay in the physical. He had tried for a long time, as we understand time, to heal his body and his soul, but the weight of his existence became too great for him to continue on this land, and so early one morning he moved peacefully from sleep through the door of death and returned to his life in the spirit.

But still all was not well, for he knew that he had not completed his purpose on Earth, and that he could not be free to move on until he had done this. So spirit communicated with spirit, and he asked his fellow band members to continue to play their music, in whatever form they chose, so that he could return to Earth through the strength and clarity of their vibrations and once again reach out to those who are his friends and loved ones, those who listen to his music and gaze at his art, those who hold him in their hearts as he holds them.

And now it is time, as we understand time, for a shift in awareness, for a deeper embrace, for a new beginning where there is no end. Just follow the music and you will see, listen to the music and you will hear, feel the music and you will know where the spirit leads.

Jerry stops. I look at the clock on the wall. It is seven-forty A.M. I have been writing without a break for nearly two hours. I hear movement in one of the beds and realize that everyone will soon be getting up. Thanking Jerry for his tale, I finish the communication with him and sit quietly for a few minutes, contemplating what has just happened. Over the past year, I have received a lot of incredible information from Jerry's spirit, but I'm not ready to do anything with it. The time (as I understand time) just doesn't feel right.

I rise and the crisp morning air penetrates my body. Putting paper and pen away, I go straight to the bathroom before anyone else can claim it. Standing in the hot shower, I reassure myself that, just as at other times in my life, when the moment is right, spirit will guide me. With that decision made, I turn off my mind and pick up the soap. Rising like bubbles in the air, the lyrics of a song that Bob often sings floats playfully through my head.

sometimes the Light's all shining on me
other times i can barely see
Lately it occurs to me
what a Long, strange trip it's been.

So true. All of this light and now I can barely see. Then a thought of recognition enters my awareness and I chuckle. Someone up there is having fun with me and I know it's all in the spirit. A smile softens my face and I start to laugh, then the laughter gives rise to song, and with water cascading down my face, I pick up the tune to "Truckin'."

Lately it occurs to me
what a Long, strange trip it's been!

The words reverberate around the bathroom, then fade away. I turn off the water, dry myself quickly, and get dressed. I shift my thoughts from Jerry and focus on getting ready to leave. The only trip I'm taking today is home.

The Other One

Excerpt from lyrics by Bob Weir and Bill Kreutzmann

the other day they waited
the sky was dark and faded
solemnly they stated
he has to die
you know he has to die

the summer sun looked down on him
his mother could but frown on him
and all the others sound on him
but it doesn't seem to matter
you know he had to die

and when the day had ended
with rainbow colors blended
his mind remained unbended
he had to die
you know he had to die

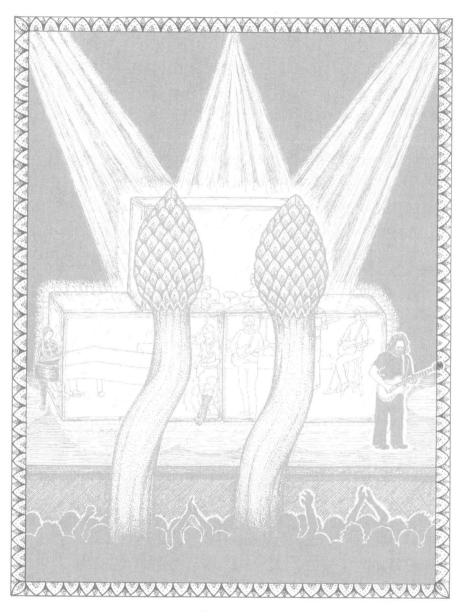

VISION

e p i l o g u e

A New Beginning

t u e s d a y,   m a r c h   3 ,   1 9 9 8

I OPEN THIS MORNING'S PAPER, AND THERE ON THE top of the front page of the *San Francisco Chronicle* is THE GRATEFUL DEAD, REINCARNATED. The article starts out, "The Dead will rise again. Playing under the name the Other Ones, former Grateful Dead members Bob Weir, Phil Lesh, and Mickey Hart—along with sometime colleague Bruce Hornsby—will band together again to head the third annual 'Further' Tour next summer."

I am not surprised by this announcement, I just didn't know when it would happen. The momentum within the band has been building for a while, but today it is official. I am very happy. It feels great. It is also the first day that has felt like spring. We have survived the winter with all of its storms, the earth is bursting with flowers, and the sunshine feels warm and inviting. It is truly a time of rebirth. The words that Jerry's spirit had spoken to me in "A Tale of the Dead" over a year and a half ago come to mind.

*And now it is time, as we understand time, for a shift in
awareness, for a deeper embrace, for a new beginning where
there is no end. Just follow the music and you will see, listen
to the music and you will hear, feel the music and you will
know where the spirit leads.*

So true. Now is the time for a new beginning where there has
been no end. I decide to check in with Jerry's spirit and hear what
insights he might have about the band's announcement. In my old
familiar way, I sit down in my chair in the living room, enter a state of
meditation, and raise my vibration. When I am ready, I open the link
with a question.

*WW: Jerry, what is the meaning of the new band's name, the
Other Ones?*

Jerry is instantly there, happy and cheerful, ready to talk. We have
become quite easy in our communication with each other over the
past few years, checking in on a casual basis whenever the spirit has
moved us. There is no formal beginning or salutation. With clarity of
voice and vision, he responds:

*J: Read the lyrics of the song. I had to die in order for there
to be a shift in the energy. My difficulty in dealing with the
physical was bringing the band down, the music down, and
the audience down. It acted as a magnet to attract negative
experiences like the ones on the summer tour.[1]*

*Now I can be most helpful because I am free to work
with the band members through their feelings and music,
to accomplish the highest good for all, to be the light at the
end of the path to guide you forward through the coming
transition.*

Birth. Death. Rebirth. It is all part of the cycle. It is

all part of life. Now there is a new beginning. It is not a reincarnation, as some have called it. It is a new beginning. We have come full circle on the spiral of life and find ourselves starting again, but this time it is at a higher level, where wisdom and experience shine clearly and we can not only see more brightly the way home, we can actually get there.

Welcome all. Look for me in the music. It is the bridge to the next dimension. I will be there, as I always have, as I said I would. The Other One—who could it be?

I laugh at the thought: "The Other One—who could it be?" We didn't know that Jerry Garcia was going to be "the grateful dead" when the band first started. Now Jerry in the spirit is implying that there is also a deeper meaning for this new name. I'm not surprised. The band is like that.

tHURSDay, JUNe 4, 1998

IT IS NINE P.M. AND THE WARFIELD THEATER IN SAN Francisco is packed to its 2,400-person capacity, with the overflow crowd standing out in the street. People are milling about, filled with anticipation, waiting for the show to begin. It is a Rainforest Action Network benefit to protect old growth forests. It is also the debut of the Other Ones.

Over the past month, everything has been in turmoil with the band. They have been rehearsing almost every day in order to be ready for this show, which is the dress rehearsal for the third annual twenty-one-city Further Tour starting in several weeks. Then two weeks ago, they decided that their new lead guitarist was not working out, and they had to hire a new one. But who? Names were proposed, musicians auditioned, but still they were unsure. With only one week to go, they made a decision. They would hire not just one lead guitarist, but two. The first was Steve Kimock—lead guitarist for the Grateful Dead–clone band Zero—whom Jerry had often praised for his exceptional musical talent. Two days later, they hired Mark Karan, a studio musician from Southern California who had grown up in the San Francisco Bay area. Once they were all together, the band had two days to rehearse. This was it. They were out of time for any more changes.

Moving through the press of bodies, I can feel the electric excitement growing in the theater. I can also feel Jerry's energy wanting to come in, but will the band be able to pull it off? Will they connect to the mystical and open the cosmic doors of consciousness for us to enter as they did in the past?

Taking my seat, I see the band members walk onstage to loud applause. Almost three years after Jerry's death, they are back together again, not to resurrect the Dead's legacy but to grow into a new sound with seeds from the past. As I look at them, Bob and Phil take their places in the center, Bob on the left, Phil on the right. On the far left, Bruce Hornsby sits down at his piano, while percussionists Mickey Hart and John Molo take their places in the back behind the two drum sets. On the right, saxophonist Dave Ellis moves next to Phil, and Mark and Steve take Jerry's old place on the far right, Mark standing and Steve sitting on a stool.

They open tentatively with "Jack Straw," then ease into "Sugaree," followed by "New Minglewood Blues." The music is good, but the magic is missing, and so is the energy from the audience. Everyone is waiting with anticipation. Will it happen? Will the band find the spark that lights the fire to lift our hearts and souls? I look for Jerry's spirit onstage, but it's not there. The momentum, the force, to bring him in isn't strong enough yet. Then I feel something shift as Hornsby plays the first bright notes of the evening. The sparks are picked up by the rest of the band and the audience responds. Soon some people start dancing and singing, but it isn't until "Loser" that the band fully connects. Hornsby, sounding like Jerry on a good day, belts out the lyrics; Bob, Phil, Mark, and Steve respond with the throbbing energy of their guitars as Mickey and John beat wildly on their drums. The musical flame ignites, the fire takes hold, and note by note a bridge is built to the next dimension where Jerry's spirit is waiting.

At first I see a shimmering white energy materialize to the right of Steve near the edge of the stage. As the music intensifies, more and more of his form takes shape, but it continues to flicker in and out. It is a young, slender body clothed in soft white cotton shirt and pants, hovering one to two feet above the ground. This is the Jerry I see in meditation. As the music opens even more, the form of a guitar appears in his hands, but the energy is still too volatile and the instrument keeps flipping back and forth. Sometimes he is playing it on the right side, sometimes on the left. I wonder if the band will be able to bring him in all the way.

Then the whole theater explodes as they slide into "Going Down the Road Feeling Bad." Now everyone in the audience is rocking and singing and moving to the beat, transported not only back to the good ol' days, but beyond. There is a tightness, an intensity, a sheer joy and ecstasy in the band that had never been there before. The momentum keeps building beyond everyone's expectations, culminating in "I Know You Rider" at the end of the first set. As Bob belts out the words "I know you rider," Jerry's form suddenly snaps solidly into place as if in response to his call. His ethereal shape shifts into his old "Jerry" body, with tousled graying hair, round, bearded face with glasses perched on the end of his nose, black T-shirt and sweat pants, and easy black shoes. As his feet make contact with the ground, his guitar stabilizes in his hands and a smile creases his face. He is back with those he loves and he is playing in the band. The Grateful Dead are no longer the Other Ones—they are the ONE.

Jerry's spirit remains onstage during the break and throughout the second set, adding to the heightened energy that is coursing around the hall. I relax and move to the rhythm of the music, letting all the joyful memories of Dead shows over the last thirty years flow into the new feelings of rebirth. A sense of euphoria washes over me, and as I gaze at the stage, a new vision appears. I am more curious than surprised at this unexpected event. The band members, including Jerry, while still retaining their individual identities, meld into a single force. Then, overlying this force, three immense translucent blocks appear. Floating slightly above the ground, two of the blocks form a base, and the third centers itself on the top. Their rectangular geometric shape reminds me of the stones used in building the Great Pyramid of Egypt. In front of the stage where hundreds of people are dancing, a field of rich, brown dirt appears. The richness of the music fertilizes the soil, and two large, green stalks begin to grow, their bright red tips, like unopened flowers, pulsing upward through the dark earth into the light. They continue to rise in undulating movements, swaying in sync to the beat of the songs, until they are as tall as the blocks. Here they stop growing but continue to swing back and forth in front of the band and the geometric forms, until the last notes are played and the music stops. The crowd goes wild, yelling for an encore, but it is twelve-thirty A.M. and the band has been playing for three hours. The show has been an incredible success and they are tired. As the powerful energy generated by the band and the audience starts to fade, the vision dissolves into air, but the spirit of Jerry remains for as long as it can, and so do we, none of us wanting to leave the incredible, transformative experience that has graced our lives this evening.

☯

Minutes pass before I begin to push through the crush of departing people toward the front of the theater, past security, and down the stairs to the rooms backstage. All of the band members are there. I feel their excitement as I enter and know that they, too, are well pleased with tonight's performance. I stop for a moment to take it all in and overhear Mickey talking to the *New York Times* music critic. "I believe that Jerry would want us to play," he says, "not to sit around and mourn forever. We don't have to do this, but it's in our veins, and it still seems like the natural thing to do."

I glance around and see Bob in a corner talking to another reporter, trying to be heard among the rising noise of voices. I am so absorbed in all of this activity that I don't even think to see if Jerry is here. Finally I decide to move on to Bob's dressing room, where it will be less crowded, but on the way I stop to talk to more and more friends, many of whom I haven't seen in the intervening three years. It is like old times, only better. There is a new, higher energy—an atmosphere filled with love and joy. We have all mourned Jerry's passing in our own way, and in doing so, we have gained a better understanding of our own selves. We are ready to leave the pain and sadness behind and move forward, both as individuals and as part of the larger family. This is truly a time to celebrate: a new trip has just begun.

I DON'T THINK OF THE GRATEFUL DEAD
AS BEING AN END IN ITSELF.... I
THINK OF THE GRATEFUL DEAD AS
BEING A CROSSROADS, OR A POINTER
SIGN. AND WHAT WE'RE POINTING TO
IS ... THERE'S A WHOLE LOT OF
UNIVERSE AVAILABLE; THERE'S A
WHOLE LOT OF EXPERIENCE AVAILABLE
OVER HERE; THERE'S SPIRITUAL
AWAKENING BACK THERE
SOMEWHERE ... THERE'S ALL THIS
STUFF ... AND WE'RE KIND OF LIKE A
SIGNPOST.

JERRY GARCIA
1942 – 1995

gLossary

Aboriginal The earliest known inhabitant of a country or region; here it refers to the indigenous people who have lived in Australia for fifty thousand to one hundred thousand years.

All That Is The highest spiritual being that exists both within and without us and from which all life evolved; also referred to as Prime Creator, God, the God/Goddess Force.

Androgynous Having a balance of both male and female energy.

Astral Body See *Energy Body.*

Astral Plane The level of subtle matter through which we pass after death. In its lower dimensions, it contains the lower or grosser elements of discarnate Earth life. In its higher dimensions, it contains productive, enlightened entities or forces that relate to the physical world.

Aura/Auric Field A subtle emanation of energy, often seen as color, from any substance; the area of the aura that surrounds that substance.

Being An entity or individualized form.

Bilma Carved hardwood sticks used by the Aboriginal people to make musical clapping sounds.

Chakra An energy center within the physical body; a wheel of light *(Sanskrit).*

Channel A person who consciously connects aspects of his or her own higher consciousness with other forms of higher consciousness for the purpose of obtaining knowledge, or who acts as a conduit for these other forms of higher consciousness.

Channeling The process by which a person acts as a channel or conduit to transmit and receive various frequencies of energy or communications with another, usually nonphysical, source or entity. This can be accomplished either by telepathic communication or by the source displacing an individual's personality to use the body as the vehicle of communication.

Consciousness Energy intelligently ordered and expressed with intent toward organization, value fulfillment, and creation; one's spiritual individuality.

Dimension A specific frequency level or plane of existence. The third dimension, which we experience physically on Earth, is based upon space and time. The fourth dimension, which vibrates at a higher frequency than the third, is where we experience our dreams, intuitions, thoughts, and emotions. The fifth dimension is where we exist in a state of oneness and love with All That Is. There is no hierarchy of dimensions (top to bottom), there are only different frequencies. It is not known exactly how many dimensions exist.

Dreamtime The beginning of time as told in the stories, songs, and dances of the Aboriginal people of Australia; a nonphysical plane where the ancestors live.

Earth Changes Earth's responses to shifts in consciousness as a result of emotional and environmental factors or influences.

Earth Plane The dimension of the Earth's physical body; that aspect of life that exists in the lower frequencies of time and space in which the illusion of form is manifested.

Ecstasy A high-frequency state of oneness with your spirit and the spirit of all that surrounds you.

Energy The natural capacity for vigorous activity; an abundant amount of life force.

Energy Body Also known as the astral body, the vehicle of the life energy (prana, ch'i) that serves as the blueprint upon which the physical body is created.

Frequency The number of repetitions of a periodic process in a unit of time, such as the number of complete oscillations per second of an electromagnetic wave.

God In a localized sense, it is an aspect of universal consciousness relative to a particular system of beliefs (e.g., the God of Judaism or Christianity); in an expanded sense, it is a collective title for that universal consciousness (e.g., All That Is or Prime Creator).

Higher/Lower Qualitative terms indicating position in a structure or hierarchy. Used here, *higher* refers to an orientation toward, or accordance with, the primary source of life (All That Is), whether referring to states of consciousness or rates of vibration. *Lower* refers to a position further removed from the primary source as manifested in physical reality. There is no value judgment when these terms are used. One state is not better or worse than another.

Higher Consciousness That part of the individual that is attuned to and aligned with the source of power and truth within; it is identified with spiritual light and awareness and is creatively expressed through thoughts, feelings, words, and actions.

Higher Self That innermost aspect of a human being which expresses its link to the universal consciousness or All That Is through thoughts, words, and actions (as distinguished from the lower self or personality of a human being); also referred to as the "God within."

Karma Unprocessed actions, feelings, thoughts, and desires that hold energy and impulse repetition of experiences until released and cleared.

Light Physical aspect: the physical vibration or form of energy detectable by the human eye. Spiritual aspect: a high vibration or form of energy beyond the range of human perception; a power or force of the spiritual aspects of life.

Mudra In East Indian classical dancing, a code of body postures and hand movements with which a dancer enacts a narrative.

Oversoul An advanced spiritual being or expression of All That Is who exists in the higher spiritual dimensions, aspects of whom have been or are incarnate on Earth or in other dimensions.

Photosynthesis The conversion of carbon dioxide and water into carbohydrates with the simultaneous release of oxygen brought about by exposure to light.

Plane A level of existence or dimension of reality.

Psychomotor Movement induced by psychic or mental action; muscular activity associated with mental processes.

Shaman A priest or priestess who uses ritual and ceremony to heal the ill (physically, emotionally, and spiritually), to divine the unseen, and to influence events.

Soul The spark of spirit existing within each individual human which holds the key to one's inner power and truth, and through which one can evolve from duality back to oneness with All That Is; the vehicle of the reincarnating individual which gathers and processes experience through repeated lifetimes; the bridge between our deathless, eternal spirit and our physical/mental body.

Spirit The individualized spark of light, the light, and the source of All That Is that exists eternally and is expressed in all animate and inanimate forms.

Totem An object or animal that is the symbol of an individual or group of people.

Vibration The periodic motion of a body or wave in alternating opposite directions from its center of equilibrium.

Ward An energy field used for protection and defense.

Yidaki An Australian Aboriginal term describing a type of musical instrument; also known as a didgeridoo or drone pipe, it is the straight branch of a eucalyptus tree that has first been hollowed out by termites, then cut to a desired length and hollowed out some more for tuning; it delivers a haunting, resonant sound; traditionally, it can only be played by men.

Notes

CHAPTER 4. TRANSITION

1. Hans Christian Andersen, "The Traveling Companion," *Andersen's Fairy Tales*. New York: Heritage Press, 1942.

CHAPTER 9. NATURE

1. Katrina Raphaell, *Crystal Enlightenment*. New York: Aurora Press, 1985.

CHAPTER 10. LOVE/HATE

1. Rosalyn L. Bruyere, *Wheels of Light*. New York: Simon & Schuster, 1989.
2. Barbara Brennan, *Hands of Light: A Guide to Healing Through the Human Energy Field*. New York: Bantam Books, 1988.

THE SEVEN BASIC CHAKRAS IN THE HUMAN BODY ARE LOCATED AS FOLLOWS:

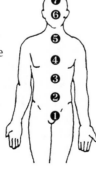

7. Crown chakra
6. "Third-eye" chakra
5. Throat chakra
4. Heart chakra
3. Solar plexus chakra
2. Pubic/sacral chakra
1. Root chakra

CHAPTER 12. MUSIC

1. Joachim-Ernst Berendt, *The World Is Sound: Nada Brahma.* Rochester, Vt.: Destiny Books, 1983.
2. Ibid., p. 159.
3. Thomas Moore, *Meditations,* p. 38. New York: HarperCollins Publishers, 1994.
4. Ibid., pp. 160–61.

CHAPTER 13. JOY AND HEALING

1. Bernie S. Siegel, M.D., *Peace, Love, and Healing,* p. 28. New York: Harper & Row Publishers, 1989.
2. Ibid., p. 3.
3. Sanaya Roman and Duane Packer, M.D., *Opening to Channel: How to Connect with Your Inner Guide.* Tiburon, Calif.: HJ Kramer, Inc., 1987.

CHAPTER 18. CREATION

1. Lester R. Brown, *Building a Sustainable Society.* New York: W. W. Norton, 1981.
2. *Sacred Symbols: Ancient Egypt.* New York: Thames & Hudson, 1995. The Egyptian goddess Nut represented the passage of the sun through the sky. Her hands and feet touched the western and eastern horizons, while her body comprised the heavens. She was the mother of the sun god Ra, whom she "swallowed in the evening and regurgitated in the morning, thus associating herself with the symbolism of resurrection."

CHAPTER 22. PROBLEMS

1. The meaning of the symbols in the *Talking Symbols* illustration: The *triangle* symbolizes the sacred trinity of body-mind-spirit. Pointing downward, it represents grace descending from heaven, water, the passive feminine element. Pointing upward, it symbolizes ascent to heaven, fire, the active male element. The *cross* represents perfect balance. In ancient times it was used to mark the way at a crossroads. It is also the mystical symbol for mankind. The *circle* symbolizes wholeness and the eternal. A series of circles, one within another, represents the cosmos. The circles also comprise Ouroboros, the snake swallowing its tail, which is the symbol of rebirth, the creation of life, and the Goddess. All of the symbols are pierced by the *lightning bolt,* the symbol for inspiration, intuition, and the life force.

epilogue. a new beginning

1. *The Grateful Dead Almanac,* Summer 1995, vol. 2, no. 3, editorial. Because of the importance of what is said, I have reprinted it here (see "A Note to Our Readers," following).

"It's got no signs or dividing lines, and very few rules to guide."
Robert Hunter (from *New Speedway Boogie*)

a note to our readers

We would like nothing more, in this *Almanac* coinciding with the Grateful Dead's thirtieth anniversary, than to say, "Having a wonderful tour, wish you were here," but alas, we can't do that. As we were preparing to go to press, there was bad news indeed from the road: First, on July 2 in Noblesville, Indiana, a mob of ticketless people trashed a Grateful Dead show at Deer Creek Amphitheatre (a Rex Foundation Benefit, no less) by destroying a fence and invading the venue, and pelting police with rocks and bottles in the ensuing melee. This necessitated the cancellation of the next night's show—the first time in the band's history that a show has been called off due to fan violence (a similar, if slightly less violent episode marred the Dead's show at Highgate, Vermont, earlier in the tour). Three nights after the Deer Creek riot, there was a horrifying accident at a campground near the Riverport Amphitheatre outside St. Louis, when a two-tiered pavilion, overcrowded with ticketless fans seeking refuge from a rainstorm, collapsed, injuring dozens, some critically. While this terrible event certainly cannot be blamed on the Grateful Dead or Deadheads, it can be seen as symptomatic of the chaos and crowd problems that imperil the fragile ecology of our community. Any threat to the safety and well-being of our fans is, quite simply, intolerable to all of us in the Grateful Dead organization.

The band responded to the Deer Creek incident with the following communiqué, which was circulated at subsequent shows on the tour.

Dear Deadheads,

This is the way it looks to us from the stage:

Your justly-renowned tolerance and compassion have set you up to be used. At Deer Creek we watched many of you cheer on and help a thousand fools kick down the fence and break into the show. We can't play music and watch plywood flying around endangering people. The security and police whom those people endangered represent us, work for us— think of them as us. You can't expect mellow security if you're throwing things at them. The saboteurs who did this can only do it if all Deadheads allow them to. Your reputation is at stake.

Don't you get it?

Over the past thirty years we've come up with the fewest possible rules to make the difficult act of bringing tons of people together work well—and a few thousand so-called Deadheads ignore those simple rules and screw it up for you, us, and everybody. We've never before had to cancel a show because of you. Think about it.

If you don't have a ticket, don't come. This is real. This is first a music concert, not a free-for-all party. Secondly, don't vend. Vending attracts people without tickets. Many of the people without tickets have no responsibility or obligation to our scene. They don't give a shit. They act like idiots. They think it's a party to get as trashed as possible at. We're all supposed to be about higher consciousness, not drunken stupidity.

It's up to you as Deadheads to educate these people, and to pressure them into acting like Deadheads instead of maniacs. They can only get away with this crap if you let them. The old slogan is true: If you're not part of the solution, you're part of the problem.

Want to end the touring life of the Grateful Dead? Allow bottle-throwing gate crashers to keep on thinking they're cool anarchists instead of the creeps they are.

Want to continue it? Listen to the rules, and pressure others to do so. A few more scenes like Sunday night, and we'll quite simply be unable to play. The spirit of the Grateful Dead is at stake, and we'll do what we have to do to protect it. And when you hear somebody say, "Fuck you, we'll do what we want," remember something:

That applies to us too.

(signed)

BILLY KREUTZMANN, JERRY GARCIA, PHIL LESH, MICKEY HART, BOBBY WEIR, VINCE WELNICK

If there's a silver lining in all this, it is the heartfelt response of the Deadhead community—you have, in overwhelming numbers, expressed your dismay and revulsion at the small, selfish minority

who disregard the common good and threaten our existence, and many Heads have asked what they can do to help. The guidelines in the band's message are a good place to start.

This scene has always run best when fueled by compassion and common sense, and we know that most of you possess those qualities in abundance. When it's working right, this relationship between band and fans has been nothing less than miraculous. Maybe now when we need it most, we can muster up a few more miracles, together.

"One way or another, this darkness got to give."

references

Barbara Brennan School of Healing

P.O. Box 2005
East Hampton, NY 11937
Tel: 516-329-0951
Fax: 516-324-9745
E-mail:
bbshoffice@barbarabrennan.com
www.barbarabrennan.com

Coral Forest

Coral Forest joined forces with Reef Relief in May 1998. Wendy Weir and Bob Weir are on its Board of Directors. See Reef Relief.

Barbara Courtney

Psychic/Intuitive Consultant
322 Meridian Drive
Redwood Shores, CA 94065
Tel: 650-595-4409
Fax: 650-508-9119
E-mail: bajeco@aol.com

Grateful Dead Merchandising

P.O. Box X
Novato, CA 94948
Tel: 800-CAL-DEAD
www.dead.net

Grateful Dead Productions

Hotline: 415-457-6388
www.dead.net

Jaichima and Vicente

Ancient Springs Retreat Center
2315 N. Page Springs Rd.
Cornville, AZ 86325
Tel: 520-639-2932
E-mail: jaichima@aol.com

Rainforest Action Network

221 Pine St., 5th Floor
San Francisco, CA 94104
Tel: 415-398-4404
Fax: 415-398-2732
E-mail: rainforest@ran
www.ran.org

Reef Relief

P.O. Box 430
Key West, FL 33041
Tel: 305-294-3100
Fax: 305-293-9515
E-mail: reef@bellsouth.net
www.reefrelief.org

Rex Foundation

P.O. Box 2204
San Anselmo, CA 94979
Tel: 415-457-3032
www.dead.net

www.in-the-spirit.com

Have you had any personal experiences involving Jerry Garcia's spirit, either before or after his death, that have deeply influenced your life?

If so, I would be interested in hearing about them. Were you listening to his music? Did he appear to you in a dream? Or did he just show up unexpectedly in your consciousness?

Please describe your experience and the effect that it has had on your life, however large or small. How did you feel? Was there a message for you? What did you learn? What was your response? Can others benefit from this lesson? Include the date(s) that this occurred, your name, mailing address, phone number, and E-mail address.

You can write to me personally at P.O. Box 946, Sausalito, CA 94966, or you can E-mail me at wweir@igc.org. All communications will be held in strictest confidence unless you authorize me to share them with others. If you would like to talk about your experience, there is a chat room on this Web site.

I look forward to hearing from you!

Wendy Weir

P.S. If you have had this type of experience with any of the other band members, please let me know, too.

about the author

Wendy Weir has spent many years as an executive in finance and banking. Her primary foci over the past ten years, however, have been environmental conservation, childhood education, and spiritual healing. She was cofounder and executive director of a coral reef conservation organization and is now on the board of directors of Reef Relief in Key West, Florida. As a director, she continues to develop environmental education programs for children of all learning abilities. She is author, with her brother Bob Weir, member of the rock and roll band the Grateful Dead, of two children's books with audiocassette tapes: the award-winning *Panther Dream: A Story of the African Rainforest* and *Baru Bay: Australia.* Wendy lives in California.